CULTURE SMART!
VIETNAM

Geoffrey Murray

Additional material by Le Thi Thu Hang

·K·U·P·E·R·A·R·D·

ISBN 978 1 85733 834 8
This book is also available as an e-book: eISBN 978 1 85733 835 5

British Library Cataloguing in Publication Data
A CIP catalogue entry for this book is available from the British Library

First published in Great Britain
by Kuperard, an imprint of Bravo Ltd
59 Hutton Grove, London N12 8DS
Tel: +44 (0) 20 8446 2440   Fax: +44 (0) 20 8446 2441
www.culturesmart.co.uk
Inquiries: sales@kuperard.co.uk

Series Editor Geoffrey Chesler
Design Bobby Birchall

Printed in Malaysia

About the Author

GEOFFREY MURRAY has worked in Asia for more than forty years as a journalist, author, and teacher, including long stays in China, India, Japan, and Singapore. So far, he has published fifteen books on a wide range of business and socioeconomic issues, mostly about China, but also including *Vietnam: Dawn of a New Market* and *Simple Guide to the Customs and Etiquette of Vietnam*, both in 1997. He has closely followed developments in Vietnam ever since he served as a news agency war correspondent with the Australian army in the mid-1960s, winning the Australian government's "Vietnam Logistic and Support Medal." He is officially listed as a Vietnam War veteran by the Australian government.

contents

contents

Map of Vietnam

- Ha Giang
- CHINA
- FANXIPANG ▲
- RED RIVER (SONG HONG)
- Thai Nguyen
- Lang Son
- Dien Bien Phu
- Son La
- T O N G K I N
- Hon Gai
- Ha Long Bay
- Hanoi
- Hoa Binh
- Haiphong
- Nam Dinh
- GULF OF TONGKIN
- Thanh Hoa
- HAINAN
- LAOS
- Vinh
- ANNAM
- Dong Hoi
- Quang Tri
- Hue
- PARACEL ISLANDS (disputed)
- Da Nang
- THAILAND
- Quang Ngai
- SOUTH CHINA SEA
- Kontum
- Pleiku
- Qui Nhon
- Buon Me Thuot
- CAMBODIA
- Da Lat
- COCHINCHINA
- Cam Ranh
- Phnom Penh
- Tay Ninh
- Bien Hoa
- Phan Rang
- SAIGON RIVER
- Ho Chi Minh City (Saigon)
- Phan Thiet
- GULF OF THAILAND
- Vung Tau
- Long Xuyen
- MEKONG RIVER
- My Tho
- Rach Gia
- Can Tho
- SPRATLY ISLANDS (disputed)

introduction

In the second half of the twentieth century,
Vietnam was in the headlines for all the wrong
reasons. War raged. It was hard to know if it
would ever end, harder still to understand
fully the rights and wrongs of the various
protagonists. First, the French tried to stem
the tide of Vietnamese nationalism; then the
United States pitted itself against what it thought
was a puny enemy, but which turned out to be
tough, resilient, and ultimately victorious. The
Americans might have pondered the fact that the
Vietnamese had struggled, eventually successfully,
for over a thousand years to escape the clutches
of their powerful neighbor, China. Patience in
adversity sums up the Vietnamese character.

Since the country was reunified in 1975, the
Vietnamese have undergone many hardships. The
immediate postwar years were extremely harsh
for many people in South Vietnam. Some fled into
exile; others underwent "rehabilitation" to make
them fit to live in a Communist state. To this were
added economic hardships and even starvation.

Today, however, life has improved significantly.
The decision to abandon one of the main tenets of
Marxism, the centrally planned economy, in favor
of a "socialist market economy" was a bold step,

as was the decision to throw open the doors and invite the world, including former foes, to invest in the new Vietnam. As a result, the economy is one of the world's fastest growing.

Visitors will find a confident, independent people, nursing few if any grudges about the sufferings caused by the war. They are open and friendly, with a sense of humor and irony, and frankly curious about the outside world. Kind and generally helpful toward strangers, they are industrious, determined to improve their living standards, relatively honest, but always ready to seize any advantage that might come their way.

Culture Smart! Vietnam is aimed at the visitor who would like to learn a little more about the history, culture, traditions, sensibilities, and modern way of life of the Vietnamese. It explains deep-seated attitudes and describes some of the social, economic, and cultural changes now under way. It dispels common Western misconceptions and gives practical advice on what to expect and how to behave in unfamiliar situations. Whether you are visiting on business or for pleasure, we hope it will enable you to discover for yourself the warmth and vast potential of this fascinating country and its delightful people.

Key Facts

Official Name	Socialist Republic of Viet Nam	In Vietnamese, *Cong Hoa Xa Hoi Chu Nghia Viet Nam*
Capital City	Hanoi	
Main Cities	Ho Chi Minh City (formerly Saigon), Can Tho, Da Nang, Hue, Vinh, Haiphong	Main ports: Ho Chi Minh City (Saigon), Cam Ranh Bay, Da Nang, Haiphong
Area	127,243 sq. miles (329,560 sq. km)	
Terrain	Deltas in south and north; central highlands; hilly or mountainous, in far north and northwest	Major waterways: Red River (north) and Mekong River (south)
Climate	Tropical in south; monsoonal in north	Occasional typhoons
Population	90,493,352 (April 2014)	Pop. growth rate: 1.06% est.
Ethnic Makeup	Vietnamese 85–90%; remainder Chinese, Hmong, Thai, Khmer, Cham, and mountain tribes	Minorities other than Chinese live mainly in border regions.
Life Expectancy	73.2 yrs.	
Literacy Rate	92.8%	
Languages	Vietnamese. English is the main second language. Some French, Chinese, and Khmer; mountain area languages (Mon-Khmer, Malayo-Polynesian)	
Religion	Buddhism, Cao Dai, Christianity, Hoa Hao, Daoism	
Government	One-party state ruled by the Communist Party of Vietnam (CPV)	Elections every five years

Economy	*Doi moi* (Renovation) policy since 1980s has created a vibrant market economy	Labor force: agriculture 47.1%, industry and services 52.9%
Currency	Dong (VND)	
Media: Vietnamese-language	Newspapers in Hanoi: *Nhan Dan* (daily), *Quan Doi* (army newspaper); in Ho Chi Minh City: *Nhan Dan* and *Giai Phong*	67 broadcasters (TV and radio), incl. 3 central and 3 local broadcasters. 75 international TV channels, incl. CNN, BBC, HBO, Discovery
Media: English-language	Newspapers in Hanoi: *Vietnam News*; in Ho Chi Minh City: *News Trove* and *Saigon Times Daily*. Main English-language magazines: *Vietnam Investment Review*, *Heritage*	Vietnam News Agency has an English-language service; Internet news sites include *Inside Vietnam*, *Vietnam News*, *Vietnam Globe*, and *Vietnam News Network*
Electricity	220 volts, 50 Hz	Flat or round two-prong plugs prevalent; British-style three-prong plugs in some hotels
Video/TV	Both the American NTSC M and French 625-line SECAM D systems in use	
Internet Domain	.vn	
Telephone	International country code: 00 84	To dial out, dial 00. Internal codes: 4 for Hanoi and 8 for Ho Chi Minh City
Time Zone	8 hours ahead of GMT; 13 hours ahead of Eastern Standard Time; 16 hours ahead of Pacific Standard Time	

LAND & PEOPLE

GEOGRAPHY

Vietnam is located in the heart of Southeast Asia on the eastern side of the Indochina peninsula, bordering China to the north, Laos and Cambodia to the west, and the South China Sea to the east and south.

It has a coastline 2,037 miles (3,278 km) long and an inland border 2,331 miles (3,751 km) long. A glance at the map will show its elongated "S" shape, measuring 1,031 miles (1,659 km) from the northernmost point to the southernmost, but with a maximum east–west width of 375 miles (600 km) in the north narrowing to only 31 miles (50 km) at

the narrowest part in the Quang Binh province on the central coast, earning the country the nickname of "balcony of the Pacific."

There are four distinct geographical sectors, ranging from rugged mountains to marshy, fertile flatlands. Three-quarters of Vietnam's territory is made up of mountainous and hilly regions towering over the deltas and narrow plains. In the northwest, there are mountains that rise up to 10,312 feet (3,143 m) at Fanxipang, the highest point in Vietnam; it contains the famous battle site of Dien Bien Phu, where France's hopes of holding on to its Indochinese colony foundered in defeat in 1954. In the northeast is the "Viet Bac"—a former revolutionary base between 1945 and 1954. The mountains then make way for the Red River Delta, an alluvial plain and the most heavily populated region in the north.

Further south are the Truong Son (Annam Highlands), regarded as the backbone of Vietnam. A plateau (the Central Highlands) also occupies this area, separating Cambodia from the South China Sea. To the south of the Central Highlands is the Mekong Delta, fertile, marshy low country that eventually becomes the mangrove swamps of the Ca Mau Peninsula, the southernmost tip of Vietnam.

Vietnam is crisscrossed by numerous large and small rivers, with a river mouth on average for every 12.5 miles (20 km) of coastline. Most rivers are small and short and are dwarfed by the Red and Mekong Rivers, both of which start out far away in China, but are navigable throughout their length in Vietnam. To help prevent flooding in their deltas, a system of dikes and canals has been erected. This has helped improve farming in the Mekong Delta by preventing the salt-water flooding from the South China Sea that used to occur especially during the long, wet monsoon season. The Mekong Delta covers a vast area of 22,500 square miles (58,000 sq. km); with fertile soil and favorable climatic conditions, it is the biggest rice-growing area in Vietnam. The Red River Delta, known

locally as the "northern delta," covers 9,375 square miles (24,000 sq. km). It has been created from the alluvial deposits carried down by two major rivers: the Red River and the Thai Binh River.

The particular geographical features of Vietnam's coast provide ideal conditions for the creation of a series of major deep-sea ports. As you travel from north to south, they are Hon Gai, Haiphong (serving Hanoi), Cua Lo, Da Nang, Qui Nhon, Cam Ranh, Vung Tau, and Ho Chi Minh City (Saigon). All the names from Da Nang southward will be familiar to Vietnam War veterans, as the ports were built up by the United States as key logistics bases. Cam Ranh Bay in particular remains famous worldwide as one of the world's most ideal seaports.

Offshore on Vietnam's continental shelf are thousands of islands and islets lying scattered from the northern to the southern end of the country. Among them are the Truong Sa (Spratly) and Hoang Sa (Paracel) archipelagos in the South China Sea, which are subject to territorial disputes.

TERRITORIAL DISPUTES

China occupies the Paracel Islands, also claimed by Vietnam and Taiwan. Vietnam is involved in complex disputes with China, Malaysia, the Philippines, Taiwan, and Brunei over the Spratly Islands. The 2002 Declaration on the Conduct of Parties in the South China Sea eased tensions somewhat but did not address the central issue of ownership and fell short of being the legally binding "code of conduct" some desired. The waters around these islands, it should be noted, are rich in oil, natural gas, and probably some mineral deposits of considerable economic worth; this provides an obvious reason, beyond pure nationalism, for the arguments.

The coastline also offers a series of stunning swimming beaches with pure white sand, such as Tra Co, Do Son, Sam Son, Cua Lo, Ly Hoa, Thuan An, Non Nuoc, My Khe, Nha Trang, Vung Tau, Ha Tien, Hoi An, and Mui Ne. In the north, Ha Long Bay, with its numerous picturesque rocky outcrops scattered over the sea, is recognized as a World Heritage site by Unesco.

Climate

Because its elongated shape crosses several degrees of latitude, Vietnam's climate is very varied. The average temperature in the north is 81°F (27°C) and in the south 70°F (21°C) and the climate is generally humid. There are clear differences in temperature throughout the year in the north, with four seasons, but very little in the south.

Two monsoons control the weather. One, which occurs mainly in the north from about October/November to March, is considered to be a dry monsoon. The other brings wet, warm weather to the entire country, with the exception of the mountainous areas, from April/May to October. July and August are considered the hottest and most humid months.

Repairing Environmental Damage

Apart from the appalling human carnage during the Vietnam War, saturation bombing, napalm, and chemical deforestation had a devastating effect on the country's forests, mangrove areas, wetlands, and wildlife. It is estimated that around two million hectares of forest and half of all the mangroves were destroyed. Large areas of the country were reduced to dioxin-soaked wasteland.

Until recently, pollution has been less of a problem than in many other countries, but as Vietnam industrializes and intensifies its agriculture to meet the needs of a growing population, levels of pesticides, chemicals, and waste products are climbing. On the positive side, the government long ago committed itself to restoring the forestry coverage to the prewar level and an extensive program of reforestation and mangrove planting has taken place to halt the serious loss of species of plants and wildlife.

As a result, Vietnam remains high on the list of countries with extensive biodiversity: 12,000 plant species and 7,000 species of animals are already recorded, including many rare and endangered species.

A BRIEF HISTORY

Situated between India and China, the Indochina peninsula has always played an important role in international trade relations and in the movement of peoples in Southeast Asia. The term "Indochina" was coined in the nineteenth century by the Danish geographer Conrad Malte-Brun, in his *Précis de la Géographie Universelle* (1810–29).

Vietnam's strategic position on the eastern flank of the peninsula attracted the attention of a succession of great powers. China dominated the scene for over a thousand years, from just before the start of the modern era until the eleventh century. Whenever China was strong it sought to continue its hegemony; when it was weak, the Vietnamese took the chance to assert their independence. It was a constant struggle that produced many heroes. By the nineteenth century, China was too weak to oppose the growing depredations of French colonialists eager to carve out a Far Eastern empire. With the collapse of French domination in 1954, it was the turn of the United States to try briefly to influence Vietnamese affairs—an attempt that ended in 1975 with the reunification of the country under a Communist government.

But how was Vietnam founded? Legend tells of a marriage between King Lac Long Quan, the "Dragon Lord of the Mighty Seas," and the beautiful Princess Au Co, descendant of the "Immortals of the High Mountains" and the daughter of King De Lai. The symbolism is important, for the Dragon symbolizes *yang* and the Immortal is the symbol for *yin*, the opposing but complementary elements of Chinese cosmology. The union of the Dragon Lord and the Princess gave rise to one hundred sons and the "Kingdom of Each Viet," whose principalities extended from the lower Yangtze River in what is now central China to the north of Indochina. The kingdom prospered, but the Dragon Lord and the Princess of the Mountains, convinced that the difference in their origins would always deny them

earthly happiness, decided to separate. Half the children returned with their mother to the mountains (that is, to China), while the others followed their father and established themselves beside the Eastern Sea (that is, Vietnam). In the third millennium BCE, the eldest son of the original union was crowned King of Lac Viet. He named himself King Hung Vuong and Lac Viet was renamed Van Lang. This kingdom comprised most of present-day North Vietnam and the northern part of Central Vietnam.

Ignoring legends, what is the reality? The first national name, Van Lang, was given to Vietnam by the Hung or Lac ethnic group, inventors of the wet rice cultivation technique and bronze drums still used today by the Muong minority. The Lac were followed by the Au or Tay Au, who arrived from the southern Chinese province of Guangxi. The two peoples integrated and formed the new kingdom of Au Lac. Following them came the Viet or Yue, an ethnic group who emigrated from the coastal provinces of ancient China around the fifth century BCE.

Etymologists and anthropologists have defined the origins of the Viet people by separating the components of the calligraphy for the word *Viet*, or *Yue*, as it is known in Mandarin. On the left side of this ideogram is a character pronounced *tau* in Vietnamese, meaning "to run," while the components on the right side signify a lance or javelin. Hence, the Viets were a race known since antiquity as a migratory, hunting people, perpetually moving and spreading beyond their frontiers of origin, carrying bow and arrow, axe and javelin. The word *Viet* is the Vietnamese pronunciation of a Chinese character meaning "beyond" or "far." *Nam* (south) probably served to differentiate between those Viets who remained in China and those who had left and headed south.

The kingdom of Van Lang prospered during the first millennium BCE under the rule of eighteen successive Hung kings descended from Hung Vuong, with a capital in the present Vinh Phu Province. At this time, King Thuc Phan governed the neighboring kingdom of Au Viet to the north of Van Lang. His desire to bring about a marriage between his daughter and Hung Vuong's son, however, was scornfully rejected, leading to protracted conflict that ultimately led to the destruction of Van Lang in 258 BCE.

Chinese Domination

Fifty years later, the kingdom fell into the hands of northern hordes led by an ambitious Chinese general, Trieu Da, founder of the independent kingdom of Nam Viet, which included much of present-day southern China. He proclaimed himself king in 208 BCE and founded the Trieu Dynasty, establishing his capital near present-day Guangzhou in southern China.

Under the Trieu Dynasty Nam Viet progressively entered the Chinese sphere of influence. In exchange for periodic tributes to the court of the Han Emperor, Nam Viet received protection against foreign invasion. This period was marked by continual intrigues, including a plot aimed at seizing Nam Viet; less than a century later, in the year 3 BCE, the Han Emperor Wudi sent his mighty armies to do just that. The country became a Chinese protectorate under the new name of Giao Chi. Highly qualified administrators were appointed as governors to rule the country, but their endeavors to introduce Chinese literature, arts, and agricultural techniques met with resistance as the Vietnamese not only guarded their national identity but fought fiercely to preserve it.

In 39 CE, a victorious armed revolt was led by two sisters, Trung Trac and Trung Nhi, but three years later, the superior generalship and weaponry of the Chinese Han armies led to the reassertion of Chinese control, which lasted until 543. During this time Nam Viet was administered as a Chinese province and a campaign was launched against the kingdom of Champa immediately to its south (see opposite).

In the second half of the sixth century, there was a series of rebellions that ended with the establishment of the third period of Chinese occupation (603–938). The Chinese made concerted efforts to establish their culture and civilization in Nam Viet, which they renamed Annam. When the Vietnamese eventually threw off the Chinese yoke, peace was cemented by the payment of tribute to the Chinese emperor every three years.

The dynasty that emerged, the Le Dynasty, decided the time was ripe to pacify the south. In 982, Le Dai Hanh launched a military expedition against the Cham kingdom, entered Indrapura (present-day Quang Nam), and burned the citadel of Champa. The conquest and integration of this northern part of the Cham kingdom brought about a marked Cham influence on Vietnamese culture, particularly in the fields of music and dance, that is still evident.

THE KINGDOM OF THE CHAMS

Champa, the kingdom of the Chams, existed in southern and central Vietnam from the second to the seventeenth century. Its culture was dominated by Hindu influences from India. Champa sometimes fought China, but was more frequently at war with its neighbor Annam. In the twelfth century, the Chams invaded Cambodia and sacked Angkor Wat, but later the roles were reversed and they came under Khmer (Cambodian) domination. Following military defeat against Annam in 1472, the Chams had to yield the bulk of their territory north of Da Nang and were eventually dispersed by Annamese invasion in the seventeenth century. The small Cham communities remaining in Vietnam today retain their Hindu culture, but larger groups in Cambodia have become Muslim.

The Great Dynasties

More glorious still was the period of the Ly Dynasty (1009–1225), which became the first of the great national dynasties under whose rule the country became Dai (Great) Viet. Buddhism flourished as the national religion and, under the aegis of Confucian administrators, a centralized government, tax system, judiciary, and professional army were all established. In 1070, a National College was founded to educate future mandarins. Knowledge of the Confucian classics and mastery of literary composition and poetry were the main requirements of the College's rigorous three-year course, culminating in a very competitive diploma examination.

The greatest achievements of the Tran Dynasty (1225–1400) were the brilliant military victories in defense of Vietnamese independence, especially those of the king's brother, Tran Hung Dao, against Kublai Khan's much larger Mongol armies. The king's sister, Princess Huyen Tran, meanwhile, married the king of Champa in 1307, helping extend the national territory southward to Hue.

Chinese control was reasserted early in the fifteenth century by the Ming Dynasty, which strove to destroy Vietnamese national identity. Vietnamese literary, artistic, and historical works were either burned or taken to China and were replaced by the Chinese classics in all schools. Chinese dress and hairstyles were imposed on the Vietnamese women; local religious rites and costumes were replaced or banished; private fortunes were confiscated and taken to China. However, a new national champion, Le Loi, soon emerged to organize a resistance movement from his village and wage a guerrilla war against the Chinese. By employing a strategy of surprise attacks targeting his adversary's weakest points—tactics horribly familiar to American troops in Vietnam in the 1960s—Le Loi managed to weaken his enemy while avoiding direct combat with the superior Chinese forces. In 1428, he founded the Le Dynasty, which lasted until the early eighteenth century, although in later years it was frequently threatened by civil war and insurrection aimed at getting rid of the corruption rife in court.

In 1788, China made its last attempt at reconquest, only to be defeated by an army led by Nguyen Hue, founder of the Nguyen Dynasty, which lasted until 1883. This event also gave the country its modern name, Vietnam. Emperor Gia Long had wanted to rename it Nam Viet and sent his ambassador Le Quan Dinh to China in 1802 to seek approval. Le told the Qing Emperor in Beijing: "The new king of the Nguyen has succeeded in realizing what the former reigns of the Tran and Le could not—the reunification of the old land of An Nam and the new land of Viet Thuong. Consequently, we would like to ask your permission to change the ancient name of An Nam to Nam Viet." But the Chinese emperor decided the name recalled Trieu Da's ancient kingdom of Nam Viet Dong, which had included the two Chinese provinces of Guangdong and Guangxi, and felt that this could lead to misunderstandings or might even conceal territorial ambitions. The problem was solved by simply reversing the order of the two words to Viet Nam.

This state now extended from the Chinese frontier to the Ca Mau Peninsula in the south, incorporating neighboring Laos and Cambodia as vassal states and with its capital at Hue.

French Colonization

French Catholic missionaries began to penetrate Indochina in the sixteenth century, but it was in the nineteenth century, during the race by various European powers for colonies around the world,

that France staked its claim to Indochina. In the 1860s, the French made Cochin China a colony and gained protectorates over Cambodia, followed by Annam and Tonkin in 1884. Three years later, these four states were formed into a union of Indochina, with a governor-general based in Hanoi; Laos was added in 1893.

Over the next fifty years, the French developed the local economy in the classic colonial manner (as an export-oriented economy that also formed a captive market for imports) for the benefit of metropolitan France. Nevertheless, they did leave behind an architectural legacy still evident in the main cities, and, culturally, created a generation of educated Vietnamese Francophones, as well as swelling the national Catholic community.

In the Second World War, with the fall of France in 1940, the French colonial regime was forced to accept a gradual Japanese takeover of the north of Vietnam in 1940 and the south in the following year. When Japan was defeated in 1945, the French moved to regain their former control, but faced an unexpected challenge from the Viet Minh, a political and military movement, founded by the exiled Ho Chi Minh from a base in southern China, which sought independence through a mix of Communism and nationalism. Although at first too weak to take on the French military, the Viet Minh gradually refined its guerilla tactics, leading to years of bitter warfare that bled France almost dry economically and politically until the end in 1954. This conflict is known as the First Indochina War.

The Vietnam War (Second Indochina War)

Any hope of peace the Vietnamese people might have entertained was quickly dashed. In the south, an anticommunist government, supported by large numbers of Catholic refugees who had fled from the north, emerged in Saigon and was backed by the United States, which feared the spread of Communism, having just fought a Chinese army to a stalemate armistice in Korea. Vietnam was divided into North and South with a demilitarized zone along the 17th parallel.

Guerilla warfare waged by the North in South Vietnam undermined all attempts to form a viable government and gradually forced the United States to take on a larger supporting role, first by providing military advisers to the South Vietnamese military and then, from 1965 onward, through a full-blown military presence. For a while the Americans professed to detect a "light at the

end of the tunnel," but this was heavily discredited by the 1968 Vietnamese Communist (Viet Cong) "Tet Offensive," which launched massive attacks on cities throughout the South. Although defeated on the battlefield, the Communists won the political battle, as public opinion in the United States turned against the war. All American forces were withdrawn by 1972 and, three years later, South Vietnam, standing on its own, was overrun by Northern forces and reunified under a Communist government.

Moving On

The Vietnam War was my personal introduction to this fascinating country. In 1966–67 I was a war correspondent with two Australian Army battalions assigned to protect the eastern flank of Saigon. The Australian infantryman proved a formidable foe, as I witnessed at the Battle of Long Tan on August 18, 1966, when a company of around 110 men, attacked while patrolling a former rubber plantation a few miles from their jungle headquarters at Nui Dat, survived an assault lasting several hours by a Communist force more than twenty times their size. The North Vietnamese were believed to be trying to overrun their base. Almost three decades later, however, old enmities have been abandoned, and in 2005 the two sides were planning to collaborate on a film about the battle.

Postwar Problems

The immediate postwar years were hard for a country devastated by decades of war following earlier decades of colonial exploitation. The French had established vast rubber, coffee, and sugar plantations to serve the export markets exclusively, but these had long since been destroyed. Imports from France had ensured that few indigenous industries emerged. During the Japanese occupation, Vietnam had been forced to contribute food, cash, and other resources to the war effort. The war ravaged the lush rice-growing areas such as the Mekong Delta; eventually, Vietnam was forced to import rice to feed itself. The loss of much of two successive generations on the battlefields had decimated the human resources necessary for national rebuilding.

THE HEAVY TOLL OF WAR

The Vietnam War resulted in about one million military and another one and a half million civilian dead on both sides. Sixty percent of the villages in the South were destroyed; in the North every major town and provincial capital, along with main roads, railways, bridges, ports, and industrial facilities, suffered repeated bombing. Fifteen million were made homeless.

For many southerners, the end of the war meant only one thing: exile. Hundreds of thousands fled, to form new communities in Australia, the United States, and Western Europe. For years after the war, the harshness of the new regime encouraged many others to try to follow them, and the tragedy of the "boat people" often dominated world headlines. Those who stayed behind, especially if they had military or political connections to the Saigon government, were shipped off to reeducation camps in remote border areas where they were forced to labor to reclaim virgin land and be indoctrinated in Marxist political thought.

More hardships followed in 1979, when a united Communist Vietnam invaded Cambodia to punish it for its harsh treatment of its Vietnamese minority under the rule of the murderous Khmer Rouge, and then was forced to fight a short-lived war with China in reprisal for the invasion of Chinese-supported Cambodia.

Economically, Vietnam followed the socialist model, but this merely made things worse and, like China, the former Soviet Union, and the former Communist states in Eastern Europe, the centrally planned economy was abandoned during the 1990s in favor of a more market-oriented system (see Chapter 8). Since 2001, the Vietnamese authorities have been committed to economic liberalization and have enacted the structural reforms needed to modernize the economy and to produce more competitive, export-driven industries. This has had some spectacular results, giving Vietnam one of the world's fastest growing economies in recent years.

THE POLITICAL SYSTEM

Just as in China, economic reform in Vietnam has moved ahead much more rapidly than any adjustments to the political structure. The Communist Party of Vietnam (CPV) is the only political party permitted, ruling under the principle of "democratic centralism." The unicameral National Assembly, or Quoi Hoc, holds elections every five years, and at the last election in mid-2002, the CPV won 90 percent of the 498 seats, while the remaining 10 percent were taken by candidates who were not party members but were approved by the CPV.

Article 4 of the Constitution of the Socialist Republic of Viet Nam stipulates, "The Communist Party of Viet Nam, the vanguard of the Vietnamese working class, the faithful representative of the rights and interests of the working class, the toiling people and the whole nation, acting upon the Marxist-Leninist doctrine and Ho Chi Minh's thought, is the force which leads the State and the society."

The CPV, playing heavily on the historical goals of Vietnamese nationalism, asserts its authority by pointing out that it alone led the nation to victory and national independence. In 1945, the August Revolution briefly established the Democratic Republic of Viet Nam before the French were able to reassert their authority. In 1954, the northern half of the country was won by Communist success on the battlefield, followed by the "liberation" of the South and unification of the country in the 1970s. Since then the CPV has claimed further victories, this time in economic terms, following the introduction of *doi moi* (Renovation) in the 1980s. Again, one can find close parallels with China in this regard.

According to CIA documents available in the US Library of Congress: "The [CPV] has presented the myths and realities of the past in a manner that suggests that they led naturally to the present. In his writings, Ho Chi Minh used classical Vietnamese literary allusions to convey a sense of mystique about the past, and he cultivated the classical Vietnamese image of a leader who reflected *uy tin* (credibility), a charismatic quality combining elements of compassion, asceticism, and correct demeanor, which legitimized a leader's claim to authority. [The CPV] has additionally promoted the importance of archaeology, popular literature, and cultural treasures in order to emphasize its ties to Vietnam's classical traditions."

Nevertheless, the CPV also had its share of failures. An attempt to introduce collectivization in the 1950s foundered on the resistance of peasants who had already suffered for decades at the hands of the French, and was abandoned. In the 1970s, the planned transformation of the South to Communism struggled to make any headway because it was entirely ideologically inspired and did not sufficiently anticipate the scale of economic and social resistance to it; the attempt to impose northern administrators on the southern

Vietnamese merely exacerbated historical resentments in the latter. Ultimately, these contradictions could be dealt with only by a degree of pragmatism, emphasizing nationalism rather than ideological purity. The need to develop a competitive market economy has inevitably exposed weaknesses in the existing structure and has gradually brought about reforms in the administrative and legal systems.

Politically, the CPV stays in the background and works largely through the "Fatherland Front" to promote "the tradition of national unity, intensify the people's political and spiritual consensus, take part in forming and consolidating the people's power, work together with the State to take care of and protect the legitimate interests of the people [. . .] and supervise the activities of the State organs, representatives of the people, cadres and State officials."

The working classes are mobilized through a state-run Trade Union, which has a nationalistic educational role in addition to the traditional functions of protecting workers' rights. There are also social organizations such as the Women's Union, Youth Union, War Veteran's Association, and various professional associations; these are supposed to play an important role in introducing government and party policies into social life.

FREE SPEECH AND OTHER ISSUES

The issue of human rights is an area that the casual visitor to Vietnam would be well advised to avoid at all costs. The New York–based Human Rights Watch in its *World Report 2005* claims the government tolerates little public criticism of the Communist Party or statements calling for pluralism, democracy, or a free press.

The government continues to brand all unauthorized religious activities—particularly those that it fears may be able to attract a large following—as potentially subversive. A new Ordinance on Beliefs and Religions went into effect in November 2004. It upholds the principle of "freedom of religion," but strengthens government controls over religion and bans religious activities deemed to threaten national security, public order, and national unity. It permits religious activities only insofar as they are conducted by officially recognized churches and organizations whose governing boards are approved and controlled by the state.

Several dissidents and democracy activists have been arrested and tried during the last several years on criminal charges, including espionage and crimes against "national security," for criticism of the government or calling for multiparty reforms. Legislation remains in force authorizing the arbitrary "administrative detention" of anyone suspected of threatening national security, with no need for prior judicial approval.

In the West, much of this is undoubtedly considered reprehensible, but one also has to see things from a Vietnamese perspective. Unifying the country after prolonged war has not proved easy, and this makes for sensitivity in high places. The war generation, heavily inculcated with Marxist ideology, may finally have disappeared by and large, but the succeeding generation of politicians still retains many of the old ways of thinking and proceeds with caution in adopting more liberal attitudes.

Nevertheless, Vietnam is certainly now a more open society, this openness being an inevitable consequence both of throwing open the doors to foreign investment and foreign tourists and of the country's membership in regional organizations such as ASEAN (Association of Southeast Asian Nations) and APEC (Asia–Pacific Economic Cooperation).

THE ETHNIC MIX

Vietnam's population is 85–90 percent Vietnamese. The rest comprise a Chinese community, and there are also various ethnic minorities including Muong, Thai, Meo, Khmer, Lolo, Man, Cham, and other mountain tribes living in remote border areas. Vietnamese is the official language, but French, Chinese, English, Khmer, and tribal dialects (Mon-Khmer and Malayo-Polynesian) are also spoken.

The Montagnards (mountain people) comprise the Thai, Muong, Mans, Lolos, and Meo tribes, and are believed to be descended from a mixture of Indonesians, Australian aborigines, Negroid Panpans of Melanesia, and other Pacific Island races. There are about two million of them in the north, with another million in the south.

Even though the majority of the one million Chinese in Vietnam were born there, they consider themselves "Chinese," and this has led to periods of unpleasantness ever since the 1950s, when the South Vietnamese government embarked on forced assimilation, which was strongly resisted. Traditionally, the Chinese have been highly successful businesspeople, and this has also helped to perpetuate the prejudice between the two communities. In Ho Chi Minh City to this day, the Chinese community tends to segregate itself in the Cholon area.

THE ROLE OF RETURNEES

Some of the Vietnamese who fled the country at various times during and after the Vietnam War to establish new lives in America, Australia, or Europe have returned home to take advantage of the more relaxed political climate, and most often to set up their own businesses. They are known as *Viet Kieu*; once reviled as traitors, these people are now treated as valuable resources, even as patriots, because of their access to foreign capital and Western business and technical expertise. The government courts them with preferential tax rates, relaxed visa requirements, even low-interest loans, although there is also an undercurrent of official suspicion that occasionally surfaces, for example in the several high-profile tax-evasion trials that have been staged since 2003. Between 1987, when the government first opened its doors, and 2003, more than 150,000 *Viet Kieu* returned to work for multinational corporations, non-governmental organizations, or themselves. There are more than

700 *Viet Kieu*-owned enterprises registered in Ho Chi Minh City alone. The *Viet Kieu* make a very significant contribution to the economy. The remittances sent by overseas Vietnamese amount to about US $10 billion, 7 or 8 percent of GDP.

If the government has been largely welcoming, not everyone in Vietnam feels the same. Some Vietnamese see the returnees as carpetbaggers who escaped the lean years and have now returned in better times to flaunt their wealth. *Viet Kieu* entrepreneurs sometimes encounter hostility in their dealings with local businessmen, and sometimes it is their own fault. Undoubtedly, some have shown complacency and arrogance, believing that their success overseas entitles them to teach their compatriots how to run a business.

Gradually, however, the rough edges are being smoothed out and there is no doubt that the returnees have played a significant role in Vietnam's growing economy. In 2001 the government eased restrictions on home ownership to allow returnees to purchase property, provided they were able to prove a long-term commitment to the country and that they would not seek to make any money out of the purchase.

VIETNAM IN THE WORLD

Today Vietnam is one of the world's most dynamic developing economies and is among the top emerging markets and investment destinations. In 2011–2013 the average annual growth in GDP was

5.5–6 percent. Annual income per capita reached US $1,960 in 2014, making it one of the countries with the fastest increase in income per capita in the last forty years. Vietnam is now a leading exporter of a number of products: the second-biggest exporter of rice, and the number one exporter of black pepper and coffee. Possessing a number of natural and social advantages, over the last twenty-five years it has attracted US $240 billion in foreign direct investment.

Vietnam now has diplomatic relations with 172 countries and has trade and investment ties with 220 countries and territories. Pursuing the foreign policy of international integration, it has been an active member of international and regional organizations and forums such as the UN, APEC, ASEM, and ASEAN, and was recently selected as a member of UN Human Rights Council. The decision to join UN peacekeeping operations is further evidence of its desire and commitment to contribute to the world's peace and stability.

VALUES & ATTITUDES

THE ROLE OF CONFUCIANISM

The Vietnamese are a people who place great emphasis on relationships radiating out from a central family core; protecting the family honor and avoiding the loss of face accompany a sense of modesty and decorum in all public dealings. Despite the recent appearance of Western ideas, China has remained the greatest single influence, perhaps understandably given its long period of rule or suzerainty over Vietnamese lands. China has imparted attitudes and value systems that

the Vietnamese classically have been taught to prize. Primarily, these have been Confucian values such as respect for hierarchy, order, and rules, an appreciation for learning, a sense of decorum and a regard for sincerity, courage,

and perseverance (the latter two values much in evidence during the war). For balance, however, Buddhist values such as compassion, flexibility, and equality also have an important role to play in modern Vietnamese society.

Until almost the end of the nineteenth century, nearly everyone lived in villages and wet rice cultivation was the principal economic activity. The nuclear family formed the basic component of rural society, although, as in China, extended family relationships were also important and relatives often lived under one roof. Ancestor worship required various religious rituals to ensure the comfort and continued support of the spirits. Confucianism demanded filial piety and obedience to one's parents, including acceptance of the parental choice of marriage partner. Women had an inferior social position and, after marriage, were expected to obey their husbands. Nowadays women are more respected in society and have taken high positions in government, such as Vice President or Vice Chairman of the National Assembly.

WESTERN INFLUENCES

Western values and behavior came in with the French, but were restricted to urban areas and to the educated and wealthy Vietnamese elite who attended French schools and adopted Western dress; the remote rural areas continued to adhere to the old ways. The tendency to adopt Western values continued in South Vietnam after the 1954 partition, with many young people seeking to emulate the ways of their Western counterparts. But social ethics in the North were dictated by Communist principles that required a fairly puritanical lifestyle and the rejection of anything considered typical of Western "decadence." The only significant social advance in the North was in sexual equality, with urban women at least freed from their Confucian fetters to leave the home and compete for jobs previously regarded as a male prerogative. Again, however, little if anything changed in the countryside.

During the Vietnam War, malnutrition and poverty were common in the North, corruption was rare, and social problems such as drugs, prostitution, and crime were limited. Modernization, however, has introduced its quota of social ills throughout the unified country. Corruption has escalated as the amounts of money circulating have increased, but unemployment is also on the rise, especially among young people. Drug addiction and alcoholism are becoming serious problems; prostitution is rampant, especially in urban areas; and there has been a steady rise in AIDS cases.

NATIONAL IDENTITY

The strong Vietnamese sense of national identity undoubtedly stems in large part from having to defend that identity against repeated foreign attempts, over a couple of millennia, to eradicate it. It helps, of course, that the bulk of the population comes from one ethnic group with a long and continuous history, although they have absorbed some foreign elements (for example, Cham, Cambodian, and, to a limited extent, Chinese) through intermarriage.

Visitors to Vietnam today will find a proud and independent people happy to go along with the notion that they are special. They like to play up the "David and Goliath" mystique to outsiders. After all, how else could they have dared to take on China for a couple of thousand years and then, more recently, France and the United States?

Although it may seem a little fanciful on the surface, some experts have suggested that Vietnam illustrates the "younger brother" syndrome: constantly pushed around by a much bigger neighbour to the north, it has been forced to display all the tenacity

and attention seeking, whether positive or negative, that typifies the behavior of younger male siblings around the world.

However, the Vietnamese have recovered from the "American War," as they call it, far better than their former enemy. This resilience is based on a belief that to remain rooted in the past retards the country's progress. It helps, of course, that they were undoubtedly the victors in their "war of national liberation."

NO HARD FEELINGS

The Vietnamese don't appear to bear grudges, or even want to raise the subject of past sufferings, as I found out on my own return to Vietnam in the mid-1990s, when I was constantly asked if it was my first visit. No, I would reply with a somewhat rueful smile, I was here (in the South) in the 1960s. The questioner would smile back and then invariably eagerly ask with seeming sincerity: "How do you find it now? Do you detect many changes?" My reluctance to mention the "W" word brought to mind the famous line— "Don't mention the war"—spoken by British comic actor John Cleese in the sitcom *Fawlty Towers* about a group of German visitors he was about to receive; but somehow the subject cropped up regardless.

One concrete example of this "politeness" over the past occurred when I met a high-ranking official in Ho Chi Minh City who smiled enigmatically but remained silent when I mentioned that, in the 1960s, I had stayed in a hotel almost next door to his present office. Only later did I learn that he had led a Viet Cong sabotage squad responsible for planting the bomb that had demolished much of the hotel floor on which I had stayed, not long after I left.

THE CHANGING FAMILY ROLE

Many writers on Vietnam have remarked on the timeless quality of the country and its people and the strength of the traditional values of loyalty and family. Vietnam has coped with much foreign intrusion, along with war, death, revolution, Communism, and capitalism. It's a bit like the traffic in Ho Chi Minh City—all mixed up but somehow maintaining a constant flow. And, in the final analysis, it is the values of family and community that hold everything together.

Traditionally, for men, the emphasis was placed on strength, good behavior, and breadwinning capabilities; women, meanwhile, were expected to show respect to men and elderly family members, while getting along with the rest of the larger kin group related to the husband and demonstrating good ability to perform all the household chores. By virtue of the principle of collective and mutual responsibility, each individual has always striven to be the pride of his or her family.

In the 1960s, the process of agricultural collectivization and industrialization in the North affected the way of life of families in both rural and urban areas, while in the South, the escalating war tore peasants from their ancient lands and turned them into refugees, leading to innumerable family breakups. The painful readjustments inevitable in the immediate postwar years, especially the disappearance of many southern males for "reeducation," did little to restore normal family life. Since the 1980s, especially in the urban areas, the changes induced by the *doi moi* policy have been most striking. Private entrepreneurship is now encouraged and facilitated. The massive development of joint ventures, especially in the southern cities, has gradually brought Vietnam into the global economy, creating a demand for highly educated individuals of both sexes.

Generational Change
Social mobility is becoming the ideal of young people. This represents a major rupture with the past, when the maintenance of the kinship-defined social position was the main objective of family organization. Success is now based on individual merit instead of family prestige,

creating new social values that have profoundly affected intrafamily and kinship relations, and contributing to intergenerational conflict.

The generational contrast is easily seen on any street. Older Vietnamese women generally wear loose-fitting pants and blouses made of silk, cotton, or linen. Many wear the conical straw hat that has, over the generations, become a national symbol of Vietnam. Young city women, by comparison, can be seen in hip-hugger jeans, halter tops, short pants, short skirts, see-through blouses, even the occasional tattoo or belly-button ring. Men and women going to the office tend to wear conservative Western-style dresses and suits.

The younger generation is open, outward-looking, and hungry for knowledge. It has embraced the American pop-culture invasion in everything from fashion to music and movies. Discos throb to the latest beat, while even the staid state-run Vietnam Television broadcasts its own version of MTV each week. Yet, despite the greater expression of individuality and abandonment of many old social customs, the young still retain one link with the past—a strong core of nationalism and patriotism.

THE CHANGING ROLE OF WOMEN

As already noted, in the traditional Vietnamese society women had no rights at all: they were not entitled to participate in the common sociopolitical activities either in society in general or in their own localities. They did not have the right to join in any discussion and decision making about the affairs of the community. Married women had no right of ownership or succession to the main property and belongings of the family, such as the land and the house. They even had no right to make decisions on how to deal with their own children. Instead, they were regarded as the property of their husbands or fathers.

The first change for the better occurred in 1945 when Ho Chi Minh issued his Declaration of Independence, echoing the words of the earlier American model, which contained the principle of sexual equality. War helped raise women's status as they were drawn into production and even into the armed struggle itself. Changes since then have included free choice of marriage partner, the right of women to work, the presence of women in public life, and equal responsibility of men and women for housework.

Women have now reached the highest echelons of poltical life as ministers—the Vice President has been a woman for decades—but there is still some way to go. Women are still underrepresented at the higher levels of government and business management. Economic modernization has generated higher levels of joblessness and the burden of unemployment has fallen more heavily on women than men. Many poor women have turned to animal husbandry and small-scale cultivation, handicrafts in the family, small businesses and services, and other occupations requiring only small investments.

Not unlike their Western counterparts, more and more Vietnamese women are opting to stay single or, via divorce, returning to that status for a variety of reasons. For women with reasonable career prospects, the lure is independence and not being tied down to household chores.

The free market economy has changed the Vietnamese family drastically. Many women have become breadwinners, toppling their husbands from their traditional positions as the heads of households. Even so, women still shoulder the responsibility of maintaining the home. And boys are still preferred, so even though the government has a two-child policy people are prepared to break the law in order to try for a boy, especially in the country.

At the same time, women who have started their own companies and succeeded, through growing self-confidence and steely

determination, often find that their husbands don't appreciate these qualities and pine for a more "traditional" woman—delicate, fragile, and yielding. Significantly, Hanoi now reports a higher number of divorces annually, compared to two decades ago. Ho Chi Minh City, meanwhile, has about half that number.

REGIONAL DIFFERENCES

Northern and southern Vietnam followed different historical routes until the early twentieth century, and this, inevitably, creates discernible regional differences. Traditionally, the bulk of the population has occupied the two bulges at each end of the elongated country. In the south, communities developed along the channels and canals of the Mekong Delta, where vast deposits of alluvial soil brought down from China made the growing of food a relatively easy task.

Similarly, alluvial deposits brought down the Red River helped create the lifestyle of the northern delta region. But, despite having vast deposits of various minerals as well as good agricultural land, the people of the north have had to struggle harder for their survival, and have known periods of famine that the south has been spared. This helped to create toughness in northerners, who have tended to regard southerners as "soft" and lazy. Such attitudes hardened during the Vietnam War, when the bulk of the southern troops proved no match for the battle-hardened northerners and required considerable American stiffening to carry on the fight.

Although the old stereotypes are breaking down today, the people of Hanoi have generally been regarded as more philosophical but more elusive when answering questions. Northern Vietnamese are also somewhat more traditional and continue to hold the extended family and the wisdom of old age in high esteem. Northerners are thought to be a bit more laid-back and calmer than their somewhat frenetic southern counterparts, for whom making money in any way possible seems to be a major preoccupation. This is perhaps understandable given the opportunities of the war period, when the economy was fueled by the powerful US dollar, and the postwar need to survive in hard times. However, recent visitors to Hanoi have detected a more materialistic lifestyle there (expensive clothing and household pets, for example), so it seems the North is catching up in this regard.

ATTITUDES TOWARD FOREIGNERS

As should by now be clear, the Vietnamese are a proud and independent-minded people. It is therefore very important to avoid situations where one might be suspected of displaying an outdated "colonial attitude." This could involve inadvertently saying or doing something that sounds condescending.

Development is uneven, so major urban areas like Ho Chi Minh City may have all the glitz and glamor associated with a major Western city, but, once one begins traveling around the country, examples of underdevelopment can readily be found. Yet much has been done, and the Vietnamese are rightly proud of their achievements and will want to seek positive opinions from visitors. Diplomacy, therefore, is a valuable attribute in one's dealings with the locals. Certainly, it helps if one has visited the country before the era of *doi moi*.

Most Vietnamese people are friendly and helpful. Foreign visitors in Hanoi and Ho Chi Minh City are often approached by young people, especially students, who want to practice their English. They may offer to be your guide without any expectation of payment.

MAINTAINING HARMONY

One should also be aware of political sensitivities. Vietnam today is in many respects a more open society than it was, but the visitor needs to be alert to the need to avoid giving any impression of interfering in the country's internal affairs in any way. Most Vietnamese want to talk to foreigners and are relaxed about this, but one needs to respect anyone who chooses not to do so, for whatever reason.

The Vietnamese place a great emphasis on creating and maintaining social harmony. Thus, they may avoid unpleasant topics or even tell "white lies" in order to defuse any potentially embarrassing situation. For the same reasons, it is often difficult to get a direct "yes–no" answer. The wise visitor accepts any detectable lies for what they probably are, and does not aggravate the situation by challenging the speaker's veracity. It can also be difficult to find out if one has done something that is considered inappropriate or unacceptable; the only way is to study the body language and to look for lack of eye contact or an uncomfortable silence.

Smiling

The smile of a Vietnamese can be very confusing and can cause misunderstandings. In many Asian societies, a smile can mean sorrow, worry, or embarrassment—the direct opposite of what it normally indicates in the West. In Vietnam, it may indicate a polite but perhaps skeptical reaction to something, compliance or toleration of a blunder or misunderstanding, or, on occasion, submission to a judgment that may be wrong or unfair.

If, for example, a waiter spills coffee all over you and smiles, it is a reflection of his acute embarrassment and not because he thinks the incident is hilarious; so it's no use getting angry in response. In fact, the waiter is smiling to try and defuse the situation as quickly as possible because he thinks the foreigner is bound to explode.

ATTITUDES TOWARD EDUCATION

The Vietnamese have a long-standing attachment to learning, and the educated person continues to enjoy social prestige. Traditionally, learning was considered more valuable than wealth and material success. Hence, rich people who were not educated were often looked down upon by others and placed below learned people who were poor. In the old social system the scholar ranked first, before the farmer, the artisan, and the tradesman. These days, of course, a love of learning does not spring from purely disinterested motives. Education represents the essential stepping stone to good job opportunities and is the prime force driving vertical mobility in Vietnamese society.

For centuries, education in Vietnam was based on the Confucian system, and, as in China, young males (no girls) studied classical Confucian texts in preparation for taking civil service examinations. Those who passed the exams were eligible for positions in the bureaucracy. The French introduced Western schooling, although few students received training beyond the elementary level and literacy

rates were low. Major advances in education occurred after 1954. South Vietnam adopted an American-style education system emphasizing the development of individual talents and skills; North Vietnam introduced mass education and trained people for participation in a Communist society. After reunification, the northern system was extended throughout the country, although technology training is now considered just as important as teaching Communist ideology.

RELIGION, FESTIVALS, & RITUALS

A RELIGIOUS KALEIDOSCOPE

Although now strictly an atheistic country under
Communist rule, Vietnam contains a rich mixture
of religions, reflecting the influence of many
cultures down the centuries. The early major belief
systems were Buddhism, Confucianism, and
Daoism (Taoism). Indian and Chinese monks
brought Buddhism to Vietnam in the early part of
the modern era, while Confucianism and Daoism
were both introduced along with the Chinese
invaders two millennia ago. All three continued
to be accepted and practiced after Vietnam gained
independence in the tenth century. Eventually,
however, the royal court recognized only
Confucianism, which, strictly speaking, is more
a set of social ethics than a religious faith.

Buddhism and Daoism, however, continued
to be popular among the mass of the population.
Christianity was introduced by French
missionaries in the seventeenth century and
Roman Catholicism in particular flourished under
French rule. There are also homegrown syncretic
religions that emerged in the twentieth century,
namely the Hoa Hao (a variant of Buddhism

practiced in the Mekong Delta) and Cao Dai, which blends various Asian and Western religious beliefs.

The current constitution guarantees the principle of freedom of worship, but the government keeps a close eye on religious organizations and activities and has shown itself ready to act against any movement that it deems a threat to national security.

Buddhism

Originating in India about 500 BCE, Buddhism finally reached northern Vietnam in 189 BCE, when certain Chinese *bonzes* (monks) took refuge there during a period of dissension at home. In the third century, more monks came to Vietnam, this time from India. Buddhism was at its height in the period between the seventh and fourteenth centuries, when various rulers adopted it as the national religion and supervised the construction of many pagodas or temples.

A decline began in the sixteenth century as royal interest waned and monks turned away from the original form of Buddhism and substituted many practices that were considered by the orthodox to be little more than superstition. Mysticism, Tantric rituals, animism, and polytheism all flourished at this time. Buddhism also came under attack from Confucianism, and continued to face restrictions during the French administration.

During the 1920s and 1930s, attempts were made to purge the religion of the various alien elements and restore a pure form of Buddhism. In the south, in the 1950s, Buddhist organizations and scholarship flourished. Buddhism emerged as a powerful political force in South Vietnam and played a key role in the downfall of the government of the late President Ngo Dinh Diem.

Today, it is hard to know exactly how many Buddhists there are in Vietnam. Without state support, the pagodas are much less elaborate than those that flourish in, say, Thailand. Young people seem less interested in worshiping than the older generation, but some authorities suggest that perhaps 10–15 percent of the population are strong believers and another 30–40 percent nominal Buddhists.

Confucianism

For those households that still follow Confucian traditions, an essential feature of the home is an altar dedicated to the family ancestors. It will be decorated with candlesticks, incense bowls, flower trays, an alcohol pot, and the tablet containing the names of those ancestors who have died during the past five generations. On the anniversary of each ancestor's death, offerings of food and symbolic votive paper clothes, money, houses, and the like are made by the head of the family. Prayers are said to all the ancestors and then to the ancestor whose anniversary is being celebrated. In addition to the anniversary veneration, ancestors are worshiped on other special days including festivals and holidays. Other opportunities to pay homage to them are major family gatherings such as weddings, graduations, or births, when reports are made to the ancestors on these happy events.

Cao Dai

This is a unique Vietnamese phenomenon of the twentieth century, created by a local civil servant in the French bureaucracy, which brings together a delightful pastiche of Buddhism, Confucianism, Daoism, Christianity, and Islam under one supreme being, the Cao Dai ("Holy See"). The sect's symbol is a single eye surrounded by the sun's rays. It  has a pope supported by female cardinals. There is also a bewildering array of saints, including Jesus Christ, the French writer Victor Hugo, Joan of Arc, Napoleon Bonaparte, and Winston Churchill.

The headquarters of the Holy See is at Tay Ninh, north of Ho Chi Minh City and close to the Cambodian border. For a while, the Cao Dai had its own army of 25,000 men and dabbled heavily in southern politics; but this force was eventually suppressed in the mid-1960s as the southern state struggled to achieve unity in the face of the military threat from the north. Today, it still exists, with many followers in its traditional areas of strength, and has come to an accommodation with the country's rulers.

The founder, Nguyen Van Chieu, proclaimed that the different religions were founded because of a lack of communication and transportation, and that all were actually seeds of wisdom planted by the one supreme God. Drawing on the various teachings of other religions, Cao Dai instructs its members to seek pure spirituality without seeking honor and riches. Members also believe in spirits, eternal life after death, heaven and hell, and ancestor worship.

Hoa Hao

The sect takes its name from a village in the That Son mountain range of An Giang province, birthplace of its founder, Huynh Phu So. He was a sickly boy in youth and his father entrusted his care to a monk who was considered to be a healer, who taught him about self-denial, spiritual discipline, and Buddhism. In 1930, the young man was said to have arisen from his bed one night and prostrated himself before the family ancestral altar. All his ailments were immediately cured and he then declared himself a prophet and began to preach. With his supposedly miraculous healing powers, he quickly attracted a following that eventually grew to more than two million.

Opinion is divided on whether the Hoa Hao is truly a form of Buddhism or not. Its founder created a simple form of worship that dispensed with the need for any intermediary such as a monk or priest and in which a person's internal faith was more important than external experiences or ceremonies. In essence, Huynh Phu So preached that it was better to pray with a pure heart before the family altar than to perform a lot of elaborate ceremonies in a pagoda.

In the 1960s, the Hoa Hao suffered a severe setback through having dabbled in southern military and political affairs (it had originally obtained arms from the Japanese invaders in the Second World War and fought on their side locally) in the same way as the Cao Dai. Its founder was executed and the sect banned for some years. Although it later reemerged it has suffered heavily in recent years owing to conflicts with the government, which has sought to eradicate its influence.

Daoism

Daoist philosophy centers on the idea of the human being's oneness with the universe. As the laws of the universe and nature cannot be changed, one should be content to live in harmony with them as best one can under the existing circumstances. This theory became popular with the Vietnamese, who have had to display a great deal of stoicism in adverse circumstances over many centuries.

In their helplessness, common people call on the Daoist priest to help them contact the spirits and delay the defeats of death and disaster. Yogic

mental self-discipline is also a part of the process
of accommodating one's self to one's surroundings
with minimum effort and discomfort. Daoism
was brought into the country by the Chinese and
enjoyed some popularity for many centuries. In
modern times, it became dominated by magic and
sorcery and now has little influence in all but the
most remote communities.

Christianity

Christianity, especially the Roman Catholic
Church, enjoyed considerable success under
French influence. Catholic communities
flourished in the Red River Delta, but suffered
heavily during the First Indochina War because of
their opposition to Communism. Hundreds of
thousands of Catholics fled the North and settled
in the South after the defeat of France in 1954.

There are claimed to be about six million
Christians in Vietnam today, with a very strong
evangelical presence. They are largely free to

worship, but there have been complaints in recent years of ill-treatment and suppression. This seems largely due to the fact that many of the Montagnard and Hmong ethnic minorities are Christian; the former have been accused of agitating for independence for the mountainous borders they have traditionally occupied, while the Hmong are mistrusted because they fought alongside US forces in the Vietnam War.

Spirits and Signs

Many of the people, especially in the countryside, believe in spirits who come in all shapes and forms, both good and bad. These are dealt with as the need arises through all kinds of ceremonies. Vietnamese also rely to a great extent on the advice of pseudoscientists and fortune-tellers when there is an important decision to be made. Astrologers predict the future by working with the person's birth date, including the year, month, day, hour, minute, and where the heavenly bodies were at that time. This conjunction is regarded as especially important in choosing a marriage date. Chiromancers predict the future by reading the palm, while physiognomists do so from the shape of the person's head.

A geomancer is called upon when buildings are being erected, for he knows just where they should be situated because of his knowledge of how invisible streams of force flow around the earth, creating magnetic fields. Buildings should be placed so as to agree with these influences. This is similar to the Chinese practice of *feng shui* (literally, wind/water).

TRADITIONAL TABOOS

There are many traditional taboos and omens of bad luck that continue to be observed to varying degrees. They include the following:

- Gifts for brides and grooms are usually given in pairs, including blankets. A single item indicates that the marriage is not expected to last long. Two cheaper items will be accepted with more pleasure than one expensive one.
- Don't express lavish admiration for a new baby, because the devils might hear you and steal the child because of its desirability.
- Mirrors are often placed on front doors. If a dragon tries to get in, he will see his reflection and think that there is already a dragon there, and will go away.
- Single bowls of rice and chopsticks should not be served. Always place at least two on a table. One bowl is for the dead. Do not pass food from your chopsticks to those held by someone else—this is part of the funeral ritual.

TRADITIONAL FESTIVALS AND NATIONAL HOLIDAYS

Tet

Vietnam inherited the lunar calendar from China, with its twelve-year cycle of years named after various animals, and continues to follow it. The lunar New Year and the season of Spring start with the Tet Festival, which usually falls in late

January or early February. Tet is a time when
everyone wants to be at home with the family.
The house will have been scrubbed clean and
decorated; new clothing will be worn; presents
will be exchanged.

Before Tet there will be a rush to buy clothing,
vast quantities of food, candles, and flowers.
Practically every family forgets thrift and buys a
large quantity of food for the Tet holidays, not
only to eat but to place on the family altar for
the ancestors. City streets are a riot of color with
flowers and decorations on each shop and sidewalk
stall. Among the items for sale are the traditional
Tet trees—pink peach blossoms in the north,
yellow apricot flowers in the south, and beautifully
trimmed kumquat trees everywhere.

All Vietnamese want to pay off their debts, as it
is bad luck to enter the New Year owing money.
In addition, Tet is a time for correcting all faults,
forgetting past mistakes, pardoning the sins of others,
and ensuring no further enmity, grudges, envy, or

malice exist. It was for this reason that the 1968 Tet Offensive launched by the Viet Cong throughout South Vietnam caught the Saigon regime and the United States by such great surprise.

A week before Tet, the Tao Quan (a trinity of spirits collectively known as the kitchen god, or the god of the hearth) ascends to heaven to report to the Jade Emperor on the past year's events. To ensure a good report, the house must be thoroughly cleaned and the Tao Quan plied with food and gifts. All the hustle and bustle of preparation comes to an abrupt halt, however, at noon the day before Tet, and everyone heads for home, no matter how far away it might be (even at the other end of the country). The first activity on that afternoon should be a special ceremony inviting deceased relatives to share in the family celebrations, and they are invited to come back for a few days and share the festivities with the living members of the family.

Huge crowds converge on city centers to sing and dance, completely blocking the streets. The climax comes at the stroke of midnight, when the Tao Quan returns to earth. In the cities, the sky is lit up by huge fireworks displays (a substitute for firecrackers, which were banned in 1995 after several deaths). People rush to gather green leaves for luck as the crescendo of noise reaches a climax.

The next morning, the family rises early and dresses in new clothes. Everyone offers each other New Year wishes, and the children are given lucky red envelopes containing money. Tradition attaches great importance to the first visitor from outside the home on the New Year. He or she is believed to influence the happiness or well-being of the family during the rest of the year. On succeeding days, visits are paid to the homes of relatives and friends.

On the fourth day of Tet, the Vietnamese believe that their ancestors return to their heavenly abode, so life begins to regain its normalcy. People visit graves on this day, acting as an escort for their departing ancestors.

Some things are considered to be very bad luck if done at Tet. One should never clean the house, insult others, misbehave, swear, or show any anger or grief. Breaking any dishes is also considered a bad omen.

Trung Nguyen ("Wandering Souls" Day)

This is the second-largest festival after Tet, and, although it falls on the fifteenth day of the seventh month, its celebration may be held at any convenient time during the second half of the month. It is not just a Buddhist holiday, but one celebrated by all Vietnamese who believe in the existence of God and of good and evil.

When a person dies, the soul will be judged to decide whether it is to reside in heaven or hell, based on the person's earthly conduct. "Wandering Souls" Day is a time for seeking a general amnesty for all souls, as well as a time when the gates of hell are opened and all the souls fly out unclothed and hungry, seeking warmth and sustenance. Food is therefore placed on altars, and money and clothes made of votive paper are burned.

Trung Thu (Mid-Fall Festival)

This festival calls for the production of hundreds of thousands of moon cakes of sticky rice, filled with all kinds of unusual ingredients, such as peanuts, sugar, lotus seed, duck-egg yolks, raisins, and watermelon seed. They are baked and sold in colorful boxes. Moon cakes in expensive ornate boxes are presented as gifts. On the night of the festival, children form a procession and go through the streets holding brightly colored lanterns lit by a candle, performing traditional dances to the accompaniment of drums and cymbals.

There are many legends related to this festival, but the one most accepted is that it began during the reign of Emperor Minh-Hoang of the Duong Dynasty. The legend relates that, on the fifteenth day of the eighth lunar month, he took his empress to a lake where they admired the moon, which is exceptionally bright in this season (China observes the same tradition), and the emperor wrote a lyrical poem.

Hung Kings' Commemoration Day

The Hung Kings were the semi-legendary founding dynasty of ancient Vietnam, and their worship reflects the belief that all Vietnamese have the same origin; it also expresses the philosophy "When drinking water, remember the source" and the spirit of national unity.

According to legend (see page 19), the eldest son of Lac Long Quan and Au Co arrived in Phong Chau Land (now Phu Tho Province) where he established the Van Lang nation and became King Hung. Van Lang was the first unified Vietnamese nation and was ruled by eighteen kings. The Hung Kings taught the local people to grow rice and chose Nghia Linh Mountain, the highest in the region, as the place to perform the rituals to the rice and sun gods. In time, a temple (Hung Kings Temple Relic Site) was set up at the center of Nghia Linh Mountain and the 10th day of the third lunar month (falling around mid-April) was chosen as Ancestral Anniversary day. From this first temple, the worship of the Hung Kings gradually spread and is now practiced both nationwide and by Vietnamese overseas.

Every year, Ancestral Anniversary day is held at Hung Kings temples throughout the land, the biggest of which is in Hung Kings Temple Relic Site. In Phu Tho Province each village selects a

festival organizing board of individuals who lead and manage the rituals. The board appoints temple guardians to tend the worship sites, instruct devotees, and offer incense to the Hung Kings year round, and villages select a ritual committee from among knowledgeable elders.

On Hung Kings festival days, communities make offerings of rice-based delicacies such as square cakes (*banh chung*) and sticky cakes (*banh giay*). People engage in folk arts and performances, including the reading of supplication petitions, praying, bronze drum beating, and traditional Xoan singing.

NATIONAL HOLIDAYS (SOLAR CALENDAR)

January 1 New Year's Day

February 3 Anniversary of the Foundation of the
Communist Party of Vietnam

April 30 Liberation Day, the day on which Saigon (Ho Chi
Minh City) fell in 1975, heralding national reunification

May 1 May Day

May 19 Birthday of former president Ho Chi Minh

September 2 National Day

TRADITIONAL HOLIDAYS (LUNAR CALENDAR)

January/February Tet

**15th Day of 7th lunar month or any time in the
second half of the month** Trung Nguyen ("Wandering
Souls" Day)

15th day of the 8th lunar month Trung Thu
(Mid-Fall Festival)

Mid-April; 10th day of the 3rd lunar month
Hung Kings

BIRTHDAYS, WEDDINGS, AND FUNERALS
Birth

Vietnamese have tended to favor large families,
although young moderns are moving away from this
trend and the government is also trying to keep the
population growth rate down. In general, boys are
more desired than girls to maintain the family line.

In traditional culture, an expectant mother was
not encouraged to attend weddings and funerals as

it was thought to bring bad luck to the families concerned, nor were encounters welcomed with people about to set out on a trip.

The longtime custom has been for the new-born infant to be dressed in old clothes, usually handed down from older siblings, because of fear that evil spirits would become jealous of new clothes and inflict an illness on the child. New clothes are only considered appropriate after rituals to celebrate the child's becoming one month old. Even then, it is not considered good form for anyone to say, "What a healthy baby," because that would be tempting fate by attracting the attention of evil spirits. Another celebration marks the first anniversary of birth. A baby is considered to be one year old at birth and thus becomes two years old when the next lunar New Year arrives. Thus, it is quite possible for a day-old child to become two years old in two days if born on New Year's Eve.

Marriage

In the old society, marriage was considered a duty to be settled by family elders. Young people readily

submitted to having their mates chosen by their parents, and they still do to a certain extent in the countryside. In the cities, however, it is easier for young people to meet and fall in love, and the parental role has been reduced to offering advice. Many still consult horoscopes as a guide to determining a good marriage partner, and, even if city people no longer place so much reliance on them, they can be helpful for a tactful premarital withdrawal if needed.

In the past, economic considerations often meant that girls could be married as young as thirteen and boys at sixteen. For the girl, marriage meant one less mouth for her family to feed, while her transfer to her husband's family gave them an extra pair of hands in the field and the prospect of more helpers through the early birth of children. In rural areas, girls may still marry in their late teens and boys in their early twenties but, in the cities, the marriage age is gradually becoming later as young people seek a good education and a career first.

On the wedding day, the groom's family and relatives go to the bride's house bringing many gifts wrapped in red paper, including betel leaves and areca nuts, wine, fruit, cakes, and tea. These gifts are placed on trays carried usually by couples who are already happily married, led by the couple considered the most successful and wealthy, in order to bestow similar good luck on the bride and groom. Normally, only the leading couple enters at first to offer cups of wine to the bride's parents; acceptance of these is the signal that all may now enter the house, accompanied by the explosion of firecrackers. The bride, normally dressed in red *ao dai* (Vietnamese national dress) emerges, and she and the groom kneel before the family altar to seek permission for the marriage from the ancestors. Following various speeches, rings are exchanged and the parents will give the newly wedded couple valuable gifts such as gold bracelets, earrings, and necklaces to end the ceremony.

Today, many Vietnamese couples, if they regard themselves as modern, exchange Western-style vows in a temple or churches, but this is still usually preceded by the traditional ceremony in the bride's home. A wedding banquet then takes place, often in a hotel or a big restaurant, during which the newlyweds and their parents visit each table to thank the guests, who respond with envelopes containing wedding cards and money.

Death

Catholic funerals follow the ritual of the Church, but most funerals are Buddhist.

The face of the dead person is covered with a white piece of paper or a handkerchief as a symbolic barrier between the deceased and those left behind. Family members wash the body with a heavily scented lotion and dress it in the best clothing.

In the past, caskets were often bought ahead of time, and in mountain areas the coffin is used in the house as a bench. In towns and cities, this practice has been abandoned. The body also used to be kept in the home for as long as six months, sealed inside the casket. Currently, it is kept at home for about a week or less.

The family then gathers before an altar specially erected in the house and makes offerings of food for the dead person's soul. This ceremony should be repeated three times a day during the entire mourning period of a hundred days. While in mourning, Vietnamese do not usually visit pagodas, festivals, parties, or other entertainments. They also normally delay marriages and do not wear brightly colored clothing. The color of mourning is white.

Funerals can be expensive. Musicians must be hired, numerous attendants are necessary, and a huge, ten-foot-high hearse painted with many dragons and other figures is used. The family engages in ritual keening, crying loudly in praise of the deceased and his or her virtues and accomplishments. Sometimes they cry over what they might have done for the deceased. Their voices, mingled with the music from the professional musicians playing wind and string instruments and trumpets, produce a soulful sound that may sound more like screeching to Western ears. When the body reaches its resting place and is about to be lowered into the grave, the wailing and crying grows more intense, and close relatives often fight frenziedly in a mock struggle with the coffin bearers to prevent them from burying their loved one. The eldest son, the monk, or a funeral attendant throws a symbolic handful of dirt into the grave and then passes on their respects to the rest of the family.

After the funeral, the special altar set up for the deceased is kept lighted with candles continuously and incense sticks are burned for a hundred days. Regular ceremonies are held for the deceased person after that time, especially on the anniversary of their death, the lunar New Year (Tet), and often on the first and fifteenth days of each lunar month.

THE VIETNAMESE AT HOME

Vietnam is a society and political system in the midst of great change. Economic reforms have introduced many aspects of capitalism to what was supposedly a Communist country (discussed in more detail in Chapter 8), and with them has come steady growth of the private economy, a movement from the countryside into the cities, and growing social exchanges with the rest of the world. Yet in some ways Vietnam is changeless. In particular, family ties remain the center of most social networks. Social modernization has not yet eroded these traditional family-based networks, although it has expanded social relations to include other networks such as those created by work and membership in various organizations.

As in most societies, it is the better educated and the young who are more locked into this wider range of social networks beyond the family, but group membership remains a desirable goal for the average Vietnamese of any age. A young Vietnamese grows up within a warm family environment, showing respect to his or her parents and aspiring to gain a good education, work hard, become successful, and bring honor to the family name.

Most people, asked if they are Communists, will reply in the affirmative, but this often means only that they regard themselves as nationalists, patriots anxious to see their country take its place among the leading nations in the world.

DAILY LIFE

The day tends to start early in Vietnam and city streets begin to fill up as early as 5:00 a.m. One reason for this, particularly in the south, is that it is relatively cool at this time, before the appearance of the blazing sun. The morning rush hour is certainly in full swing between 6:00 and 7:00 a.m. Many commuters stop at street stands or small restaurants to eat a hurried breakfast rather than have breakfast at home, thus saving both shopping for the ingredients and time spent in preparation.

Schools open at 7:00 a.m. as well. Those who have the time to spare, including housewives, head for the markets to buy the fresh meat and vegetables that will be put on the table later in the day. The traditional markets are noisy, chaotic places filled with the chatter of furious bargaining over the produce, which will have been brought in well before dawn by peasants from outlying areas. In the cities nowadays, however, supermarkets and mini-marts provide a quieter alternative—at a price—and also offer some foreign products.

Because of the early start, lunch is also taken early, around 11:00 a.m., after which those who can will escape the hottest time of the day with a quiet nap. The lucky ones can do this in air-conditioned comfort these days, but for many people the only breeze is provided by a ceiling or portable fan.

An average family normally dines around 6:00 p.m. and then settles down on weekdays to watch television or engage in some other leisure activity. For many, this will involve an after-dark stroll around town in the cooler air or, increasingly, a ride on the family motorcycle, perhaps with the addition of a movie or a stop for a drink in a sidewalk café. Although life in the streets never seems to settle down, most families cannot afford to keep late hours given their early rising time.

Life in recent years has certainly become more comfortable for some segments of the population, with more money available to provide many of the basic "comforts," such as television sets, refrigerators, or electronic goods (see opposite).

WHO SPENDS WHAT

As a result of economic progress family life in the cities has improved in recent years. A government survey in 2014 found that while only 1.8 percent of households owned a car, 115.3 percent owned a motorbike, that is, some had more than one. (You may think they are all on the road at the same time during rush hours!) Virtually all households owned a television set; 18.8 percent had a computer; 49.7 percent had refrigerators; 11.6 percent air conditioners; and 22.7 percent washing machines.

In the countryside the figures were naturally lower, with fewer households having a television set. The bicycle was the main mode of transport, with 91.9 percent of households possessing one or more bicycles, but only 13.9 percent motorcycles. In the countryside, when there is some money to spare, the tendency is to invest in expensive furniture rather than the electrical goods favored by city dwellers.

There are significant differences in the spending behavior of families from region to region. In the plains, families spend 51 percent and in the highland areas 60.1 percent on food each day. Urban families, however, spend only 36.7 percent of their total income on daily meals, which can be explained by their larger income potential. Obviously, in a country that is still relatively poor, the household economy tends to cater to only the most essential needs. The social structure in which extended families with several members working outside the home is the norm, however, does mean that income can be pooled for major purchases.

Spending on clothing has also seen major growth. Bogus versions of Levis and Calvin Klein jeans were available in the local markets for years, but local production of the real thing began in the mid-1990s. High-class Western clothes shops have been evident in Ho Chi Minh City since the 1990s, as southerners, with their greater exposure to Western culture, are very aware of the significance of branding. Hanoi residents were slow to catch up, but, as we have seen, have finally done so, at least in the wealthier neighborhoods of the capital. In both Hanoi and Ho Chi Minh City there are luxury shopping malls selling internationally known brands such as Gucci and Louis Vuitton.

In 2014, 71,045 cars were imported, whereas 128,000 cars were assembled or manufactured in the country. The latest versions of Rolls-Royce, Jaguar, Bentley, and Lamborghini have all been introduced into Vietnam.

HOUSING

At present, in Vietnam, an estimated 15 million people—a fifth of the total population—live in urban centers, the majority of them in Hanoi and Ho Chi Minh City. Rapid growth in the urban population has put great pressure on the ability of the cities to provide sufficient decent housing. The government has been anxious to hold down the growth of the major cities and to spread the population more evenly around the country.

Ho Chi Minh City is the largest and fastest-developing city, with a population of about

8 million in 2014; there were no households living below the official poverty line in that year (nationally, the figure was 6 percent). The old slum areas that had sprung up beyond the charming inner city area by the Saigon River during the war have now been removed and replaced by new, low-cost government housing.

There are a number of new property developments in both Hanoi and Ho Chi Minh City with international standard facilities: Saigon Pearl by the Saigon River, Diamond Island, Phu My Hung in Ho Chi Minh City, or Ciputra, Ecopark, and Vincom in Hanoi. High-end apartments here cost between US$ 1,700 to US$ 5,000 per square meter. The investors are mainly foreigners and Vietnamese. Vietnam was also affected by the global "real estate crisis" of 2008, and the property market is still stagnant—though this is good news for medium-income purchasers of apartments.

The office and business buildings in Hanoi and Ho Chi Minh City are much the same as in New

York, Hong Kong, or Singapore: Bitexco Financial Tower in Ho Chi Minh City with 68 storeys and a height of 262.5 meters (100 percent Vietnamese investment); Keangnam Hanoi Landmark with 71 storeys and a height of 350 meters (South Korean investment); Lotte Center Hanoi with 65 storeys and height of 272 meters.

In the North, constant bombing raids during the war demolished many urban areas, with Hanoi and Vinh two of the main victims, requiring a major postwar reconstruction program in newly created outer suburbs. In Hanoi's inner city area, many of the delightful villas from the French colonial era have been saved and renovated for rental or resale, although only foreign businessmen working with big corporations or rich returning Vietnamese tend to be able to afford them.

Living conditions, therefore, vary widely; but, for the majority of urban people the reality is cramped, functional housing lacking in privacy. In mountainous and remote rural areas many people still live in fairly poor conditions, lacking many of the most basic amenities.

THE EDUCATION SYSTEM

Most of the adult population is literate (92.8 percent in 2014). Education is free and is compulsory for five years of primary school, but the rate of school attendance for secondary education falls off rapidly outside the cities, especially in the mountainous areas of the country and particularly among girls.

There are nearly 22 million students in the education system and 1.2 million teachers and instructors. The structure of the school system is "5–4–3", that is, five years of primary education (grades 1–5) followed by four years of lower secondary (grades 6–9) and three years of upper secondary (grades 10–12). Higher education programs last between two and six years.

In 1993, the government reorganized higher education to improve the system's overall ability to educate students in the principles of a market economy and train them to meet the changing needs of the labor market. By 2001, about one-tenth of those of relevant age were involved in higher education. Major universities are located in Hanoi, Hue, Thai

Nguyen, Da Nang, and Ho Chi Minh City, and the provincial capitals have smaller institutes. Today there are 376 colleges and universities in the country.

Spending on education commands a significant portion of the state budget. In the mid-1990s, it was about 12 percent, but the figure rose to 16.85 percent in 2012.

One other significant change in this period has been the removal of many of the old restrictions on the private sector's involvement in education. So-called "semi-public" and "people-founded" institutions have rapidly increased in number; nonpublic education is especially common in preschool, vocational, and technical education, and increasingly also at the higher level of general education. Such institutions cover nearly all of their operating costs from student fees.

A foreign education is becoming more popular with each passing year. In 1993 Harvard University set up a Fulbright Economic Teaching Program in Ho Chi Minh City, teaching the fundamentals of the market economy and public policy to Vietnamese middle managers. Today international universities in the country include RMIT (Australian) and British University Vietnam. Some Vietnamese institutions have joint programs with foreign universities that enable their students to complete their final year at universities in the US, UK, Australia, and New Zealand.

The number of Vietnamese studying abroad has been growing and is about 60,000. Top countries for Vietnamese students include the US, China,

Australia, the UK, and Japan. At the last count there were more than 16,000 Vietnamese students in the USA.

MILITARY SERVICE

Every able-bodied male is expected to make himself available for military service and must register for it upon reaching the age of seventeen (or at sixteen voluntarily), although the actual draft age is from eighteen to twenty-seven. Women can also volunteer. At present, on average, almost a million youths "come of age" every year. At the time when Vietnam still seemed to be on a war footing after reunification (because of the war in Cambodia), male conscription was universal, although attempts were made to encourage voluntary enlistment by offering enlistees opportunities for advancement and the acquisition of additional skills that would improve their job prospects upon returning to civilian life. Combined with Party membership, military service is certainly a means of career advancement in the public sector.

Service in the People's Army of Vietnam (PAVN) is considered a great honor, and for years many southerners were excluded because their political background was considered suspect. With the onset of more peaceful times, the draft gradually became more selective and greater reliance was placed on voluntary enlistment (even if different areas were given quotas to fulfill as best they could).

VISITING A VIETNAMESE HOME
What are the opportunities for the foreigner
to view Vietnamese home life firsthand?
Vietnamese people are not particularly highly
paid and for the ordinary citizen it is often a
struggle to make ends meet. Despite this, they
like to be hospitable and one should treasure
any invitation that has been issued to "come
home for dinner," as these are not issued lightly.
Before taking up the invitation, however, it is a
good idea to understand a few facts of life about
Vietnam today and the struggles of its people to
create a better standard of living for themselves.

The Vietnamese enjoy being good hosts, and
should be allowed to do so, even if it seems that

 they have been
stretching their
own (and others')
resources to put on
a good show.
Certainly, one
should never offer
to share the costs—
simply make a silent vow to reciprocate in a
good restaurant at the first opportunity.

Of course, getting an invitation into a
Vietnamese home is not going to happen
immediately after you arrive, and you should
not strive too hard to get one. The best tip is to
let the Vietnamese take the initiative—if they
feel comfortable issuing an invitation, that's fine.
It may be hard for them to understand that, no

matter how humble the surroundings, you really would prefer to relax in a homey atmosphere than to have yet another meal in yet another impersonal restaurant.

Unless the friendship is very close, it would be unwise to drop in on a family uninvited, as this could cause embarrassment that the house is not tidy enough or no preparations have been made to feed and otherwise entertain the guest. Equally, it is not wise to make casual calls around lunchtime or early afternoon, when people may be enjoying the traditional siesta.

Making a Good Impression

Turning up with a gift, or gifts, is not absolutely essential, but if you do, then these should be items that the family could not easily obtain themselves. To take something that the hosts could buy easily would be a bad reflection on their economic means. The Vietnamese love anything foreign, and it does not have to be expensive. If you bring the children presents, each child should have its own. Also remember that, if the gift is wrapped, it is unlikely to be opened in the presence of the giver as this is not considered polite.

Your host may come to collect you from your hotel for the occasion, but if you are to be trusted to find your own way and are a little unsure of the location, a dry run might not be a bad thing, so as to make sure you can reach your destination on time regardless of traffic conditions.

Etiquette on Arrival

On entering the home, drink the tea that is invariably offered, even if you don't like it; the fact that it is being served shows that you are welcome and well respected. One is not obligated to drink the offering beyond a few sips—in fact, an empty cup or glass usually obliges the host to fill it up again! Snacks may be served and these can be sampled in moderation, but should not be allowed to impair the appetite for the meal to follow.

Social rank, especially within the family, may no longer be as important as before, but it is always wise to be alert to any nuances in this regard. Certainly, it would be respectful to greet the older members of the group first and then work down to the youngest. For modes of address, see Chapter 9, "The Naming System."

Table Manners

The etiquette of dining will be dealt with in more detail in the next chapter, but if you are invited to partake of a home meal, here are a few points worth mentioning at this stage:

Wait for the host to indicate where you should be seated, which will certainly be in a position considered the most comfortable in the whole room (well away from drafts and kitchen smells).

If the dinner is served in the Chinese style, food should be transferred from the main bowl to your individual bowl before eating. It is impolite to eat anything with your chopsticks directly from the serving bowl.

You may refrain from taking something you
don't like, but, if the hostess serves it to you
unknowingly, force it down if at all possible.

Certain foods, such as chicken's head or
feet, are considered great delicacies and will be
offered as a matter of course to the honored
guest, and a certain amount of diplomacy and
fortitude is needed in handling these situations
(remember, your host would love to eat the item
on offer!).

Individual bowls are usually changed with
each course and are generally removed only
when empty, except for the last course. Here,
a little something should be left in the bowl to
indicate to the host that there was enough
food and everyone is satisfied.

chapter five

FOOD & DRINK

FOREIGN INFLUENCES

Vietnamese cooking, while possessing a unique style all its own, has been heavily influenced by the traditions of its neighbors. Stir-frying, deep-frying, and even chopsticks were introduced from China centuries ago and became embedded in northern culinary culture; the southern part of the country was influenced more by Cambodia, Thailand, and India for historical reasons. But, although the ingredients are the same, southern Vietnamese food is more subtle and less overwhelmingly spicy.

Foods such as bamboo shoots, bean curd, lotus roots or nuts, bean sprouts, Chinese cabbage, water spinach, and kale will be familiar to anyone who has traveled in Asia before. Vietnamese cooking, however, depends heavily on a wide range of fresh herbs to provide distinctive flavors. Emphasis on fresh ingredients and the minimal use of fat in cooking preparations have also given the cuisine a healthy reputation.

The French Legacy

The French colonial period has left behind a legacy of wonderful fresh-baked bread. An

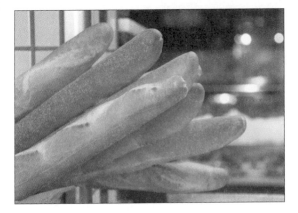

excellent cheap and satisfying meal, for example,
is a fresh baguette filled with salad, local pâté,
cheese, or, especially at breakfast time, butter and
jam. Even in the smallest towns, one can usually
find vendors selling crispy bread rolls filled
perhaps with ground pork and herbal seasoning.
The croissant is also popular at breakfast.

A fondness for coffee is apparent throughout
the country and small cups of *café filtre* are
especially popular in the south.

EATING OUT

Eating out is a way of life, especially with so many
wives working these days and homes tending to
be somewhat small for handling many visitors.
It makes sense to form a large party in order to
enjoy a Vietnamese meal to the full. The idea is
that a large number of varied dishes, reflecting
a full range of tastes, textures, and cooking

techniques, should be ordered and placed in the middle of the table for communal dining.

Westerners, who might normally expect to eat their food along with a bowl of rice, as happens in Japan for instance, will find that Vietnam tends to follow the Chinese custom of serving rice at the end of the meal. But it is possible to ask for it to be served earlier.

Vietnamese restaurants around the country range from tiny, street-side *pho* stands offering a noodle-based soup that is standard fare for many Vietnamese, especially in the North, to the most opulent establishments targeting foreign visitors and well-heeled Vietnamese. The soup in the *pho*, incidentally, is normally made from oxtail or beef stock, lavishly seasoned with a variety of spices and herbs, including crushed chilies, ginger, cinnamon, and star anise. In the North, thin strips of raw beef are likely to be added.

Many hotels and restaurants specialize in providing a comprehensive, banquet-style meal, specifically aimed at tourists who wish to sample different foods from around the country under what might be delicately called "controlled conditions." Other restaurants cater to a more select clientele, offering perhaps one or two specialties, but at a price. There are plenty of Western-style restaurants, including the ubiquitous fast-food outlets seen all over the world.

The more adventurous visitor, however, can plunge into the backstreets of Hanoi or Ho Chi Minh City to discover hole-in-the-wall establishments offering authentic cuisine at low prices. Language may prove a slight problem in such places, but pointing at what is on the plate of fellow diners is a good substitute. However, as fresh, raw vegetables are a major part of many Vietnamese dishes, it might be wise in some of the less well-appointed eating places to check that all the ingredients have been thoroughly washed.

Popular Dishes
Anyone familiar with Chinese takeout will relish the Vietnamese spring rolls (*nem* in the north and *cha gio* in the south) filled with shrimps,

vermicelli, chopped onion, and mushroom, which tend to be thinner and more delicate than their Chinese counterparts.

Among meats, pork and chicken dishes tend to abound because both animals are bred in large quantities, unlike beef, which tends to be expensive for the opposite reason. However, the deadly bird flu has heavily affected the chicken population in recent years. The best way to eat meat dishes is to find a restaurant where you can barbecue the meat over a charcoal burner yourself, adding extras to taste from a vast plateful of herbs and vegetables, such as lettuce, onion, mint, basil, parsley, and red and green peppers. Western visitors accustomed to eating only chicken breasts should be warned that Vietnam follows the Chinese style of including everything—bone, gristle, and various dubious-looking internal organs. In fact, some of the bits

Westerners might normally discard, such as the feet, are highly prized delicacies.

Especially popular in the northern winter is what is known elsewhere in the region as "steamboat" or "Mongolian hotpot" and is here called *lau*. A large bowl filled with seasoned broth is placed on a charcoal brazier and meat and vegetables are then added to it by the cook or individual diner. Apart from meat, fish is also used.

Given Vietnam's long coastline and many rivers, fresh fish is plentiful and cheap. The giant prawns, cuttlefish, and crabs are delicious, even more so when they can be selected live from a tank inside the restaurant. Eels are also popular. One of the best fish dishes is *cha ca* (grilled fish with dill).

Ho Chi Minh City has always been regarded as the gastronomic capital of the country and

it retains this label today, despite some improvements in Hanoi. The sultrier climate in the south encourages outdoor eating, and one can start off early in the morning with *xoi* (sticky rice) from a street corner stand, perhaps followed by some form of noodles and washed down with hot, fresh soy milk. For lunch, a good eating experience is to be found at the food stands of the downtown Ben Thanh Market. Again noodles might be a good choice, such as *bun bo Hue* (Hue-style beef noodle soup) and *mi quang*, a turmeric-tinted flat noodle served with pork, shrimp, toasted rice paper, fresh herbs, and a sauce made with minced pork. For dessert, one might try a pudding made of coconut milk and bananas, or cooked fruits and dumplings.

At night, one might plunge down a promising alleyway in search of tiny outdoor restaurants serving *banh xeo* (rice-flour crêpes), thin and

crispy and cooked in a blazing hot wok, the thick clouds of smoke and delicious aromas helping to sharpen the appetite. Traditionally, they are made with shrimp and pork, but any combination of meat and vegetables will work. To enjoy this dish the traditional way, tear off a piece of crêpe, wrap it with lettuce (or mustard greens) and herbs, then dip it in *nuoc mam* sauce.

The Importance of *Nuoc Mam*

Many sauces are provided with most meals, including soy sauce and chili sauce. But the most ubiquitous is *nuoc mam*, often described as "rotten fish sauce" and a bit disconcerting for the first-time visitor. *Nuoc mam* is indeed a fish-based sauce, unique to Vietnam, and is considered an essential accompaniment to most meals.

It is prepared from various species of fish that are mixed with salt and then left to liquefy in wooden barrels for several months—the longer the brewing period the finer the sauce and the higher the price. It can be used alone as a dip, or mixed with garlic, chili, sugar, vinegar, and fresh lime, when it is known as *nuoc cham*. One way to tell if you have got good *nuoc mam* is to check the color. If it is dark brown, it is certainly of inferior quality; top class sauce should be almost like oil and light yellow in color.

Drinks Hard and Soft

There is a plentiful choice of drinks to accompany a meal. Locally brewed beers, often major foreign brands produced under license, abound. Among the domestic brands, the best known in the south is 333, whose notorious use of formaldehyde as a preservative can result in a pretty nasty hangover. In the north, Hanoi beer is the most popular brand. *Bia Hoi*, or fresh beer, is worth sampling in the big cities. Wine is fashionable among the Westernized middle-classes in the big cities, mostly imported from Chile and France. Viticulture was started by the the French in colonial times, and today Vietnam produces its own wine called Da Lat, after the central highland area where the grapes are grown.

There are also some potent local liquors, notably a rice wine called *ruou de* in the south, which is similar to Japanese saké and has the same lethal effect on the legs unless approached with caution. In the north it is called *ruou quoc lui* (literally "state hide") because in the past it used to be produced illegally by individuals and families for their own use. Whiskey is popular among the young in bars and discos in the cities.

Drinking water outside the major hotels should be approached with caution; bottled, purified, or mineral water is a wiser option. However, be careful when buying branded water as many local imitators have sprung up, using almost identical bottle shapes and labels, to confuse the consumer into drinking ordinary tap water.

TRADITIONAL HABITS

The custom of chewing betel and areca nuts has a history stretching back many centuries in Vietnam, although it now tends to be restricted to rural areas and especially the elderly population. A betel nut chewer invariably displays a mouth stained bright red. Old medical books insist that the benefits include leaving the mouth fresh and fragrant, helping to reduce bad temper, and easing digestion. A wad of betel consists of four materials that create a sweet, bitter, hot, and pungent taste. At any wedding ceremony, there must be a dish of betel and areca nut for guests to share; during funerals, it can help relieve sadness. In the worship of the ancestors, betel and areca nut must be present on the altar.

While walking around city streets, one often comes upon a low table with glass pots containing different kinds of candies, roasted peanuts, and sugarcoated cakes; next to them is a tea pot and a tray of cups. Around the table are several small wooden stools. This is a makeshift tea shop, a very popular part of Vietnamese street life. Tea is considered indispensable to every inhabitant of the city, being drunk repeatedly every day from the early morning until late at night. People drink tea at their homes, at their workplaces, and even in tea shops on their way to and from work.

Whenever the Vietnamese feel thirsty, they are likely to look for this drink. It is drunk in both the summer and the winter months. In the winter, a sip of hot tea makes you feel warm inside and better able to cope with the cold temperatures outside. Unlike northerners, whose preference is for a cup of hot steamy tea, people in the south tend to add ice cubes for a cold drink.

TIPPING

Officially, tipping is not allowed, but that does not stop tips being sought. However, one should be aware that hotel restaurants in particular tend to add a service charge, and restaurant bills in general are also subject to government tax. At the same time, some restaurants charge an additional 5–10 percent for payment by credit card. All these extra charges certainly act as a disincentive to generous tipping!

In small eating places where it's going to be a straight cash transaction, one could round up the bill to an appropriate amount and wave away any attempt to proffer change. The same applies to tips for taxi drivers. Naturally, the average Vietnamese worker would welcome any supplement to his or her basic pay in recognition of what you would consider conspicuously good service (and the tip is a way of ensuring that this service continues to be offered).

BANQUETS AND ENTERTAINING
Eating Breaks the Ice
Eating and drinking are a major part of doing business in Vietnam. Dinners with local agents

and customers help to develop networks and cement relationships. During business negotiations, for example, they offer the two sides a chance to size each other up and discover the human beings behind the negotiating masks. They can help break the ice when the two sides are not familiar with each other.

These occasions tend to be fairly informal, much more so than their equivalents in, say, Japan. Toasting at banquets and after-dinner activities such as singing are common practices.

Be in Good Voice

It has been my experience gained through many years in Asia that most people are good singers and have an extensive repertoire. The poor Westerner is often put to shame by his own lack of ability to sing well or even remember the words of a song. I have often been embarrassed, for example, after my hosts have delivered a selection of traditional love songs in beautiful tenor voices, to be reduced to something like "You are my sunshine, my only sunshine ..." In desperation, I eventually memorized a local song, and was quite a hit!

Speeches, if any, should be fairly light, avoiding business and politics, and humor should be avoided as jokes don't usually translate well into another culture. Sincerity and friendliness are the two aspects that should come across most strongly. How one performs at a banquet can often help dissolve differences and bring an agreement much closer. You can, for example, toast a project's future success, express your happiness at being in Vietnam, or say how glad you are that you are working with the other party. It is customary to applaud your own speech.

Vietnamese men often smoke during the meal, political correctness regarding smoking having not yet reached this part of the world. Smoking is prohibited in government offices.

Toasting

When cognac or whiskey is served—which can be at any time during the meal—the custom is for individuals to drink only after a toast is made. Returning a toast is standard practice. Common toasts are "*Tram phan tram*" ("Empty your glass, 100 percent") and "*Chuc suc khoe*" ("Good health").

Return Match

Apart from business occasions, one should also arrange a meal at a good restaurant to return any invitation from a family to dine in their home. If you are the one organizing the banquet, take care with the seating to ensure there are no gaffes over seniority in rank or age. Ensure that your guests are invited to eat when each course is served. Keep an eye open for empty glasses and make sure they are refilled with the drink for which the individual has demonstrated a preference.

Invitations and Arrangements

For large and important functions where guests are invited from various organizations, it is advisable to telephone and check whether they have received your invitation and will attend the function, because many Vietnamese are not yet used to the practice of confirming invitations.

In preparing to host a formal banquet, especially if it is your first time, it would be wise to take advice from a local. For instance, what type of restaurant should you choose? If at the top end of the scale, will it impress your guests or merely intimidate them? (Remember there is a difference between business and family entertaining.) What dishes and what liquor should be ordered, again to create a good impression? What about seating arrangements?

DINING ETIQUETTE

If you are the guest of honor at a dinner, you may find yourself being treated somewhat like a baby: someone else serves your food for you, or, at least, the host sees to it that the guest has the first sampling of each dish. The drawback of this, as we have seen, is that one can be served something of unknown origin and not necessarily suited to the foreign palate. In such a case show fortitude and swallow the tidbit with good grace, knowing that it is being offered out of a sense of friendship and good manners.

Sampling probably best sums up Vietnamese dining; one should try a little something from every dish on the table as it arrives and not dwell on any dish for too long. Express a good opinion of each dish in turn and show a lively interest in how it is prepared and whether it is a regional specialty.

Whereas it might be regarded as impolite to ask for "seconds" in the West, in an Asian society such as Vietnam, eating to repletion and even beyond is considered a polite way of expressing satisfaction with the food on display. To eat sparingly, even if you are on a diet, is to suggest either that the cook lacked skill or that the host lacked ability in selecting a good restaurant or choosing the best dishes.

CHOPSTICK SKILLS AND ETIQUETTE

Doi dua is the Vietnamese word for what Westerners called "chopsticks," and a demonstration of skill in handling these implements will invariably draw compliments from your fellow diners. But there are a host of rules of etiquette that govern their use, and failing to abide by them will quickly lower that initial good opinion.

It is generally considered more elegant to hold the chopsticks as far away from the business end as possible. This naturally requires more dexterity, so a child will normally hold them much lower down and then gradually work backwards with gathering experience. There is an old superstition that to hold chopsticks halfway down is actually a harbinger of a family death. In some situations, however, it is customary to do so if the eater wishes to use both ends alternately—the blunt end to pick up food from a communal dish and place it in the individual's bowl, and the tapering end for depositing this food in the mouth.

Chopsticks should not touch the lips, teeth, or tongue. Never pick up more than one morsel with them. It is also not polite to move food from the communal plate directly to the mouth; instead, it should be transferred to your own bowl. It is considered very distasteful to shift the food about on the serving plate in search of a choice item—and even more so to return it to the plate as unacceptable! Morsels should not be picked up by piercing them with the chopstick. The food should be picked up quickly with as much dexterity as you can manage (not easy if it is a greasy item that is sliding around; some thought should be given in advance as to how one should tackle this problem).

If all else fails, you can ask for a fork. In addition, Vietnamese use deep ceramic spoons especially for soup.

TIME OUT

Vietnamese people don't have too much leisure time.
There are few national holidays on which they can
relax, and generally it is more the traditional festivals
that give them a chance to let their hair down. Eating
out is an important social activity and a chance to
unwind, and there is a great deal of social intermingling
through visits to the homes of families and friends.

Sports are starting to take hold today, and both
the men's and women's national soccer teams have
large followings. As far as participation is concerned,
the various martial arts, basketball, and volleyball
have all gained in popularity in recent years; on a
more sedentary note, chess is widely played. Most
Vietnamese belong to some form of social organization
and these open up new options for friendship and
extramural activities.

But there is also a rich and ancient national culture
that is available to all and is widely appreciated.

VIETNAMESE CULTURE
Music and Theater
In the musical and theatrical arts, Vietnam originally
was much influenced by China, but went on to
develop some unique forms of its own. Young

people today do not have the same intense interest in traditional music as previous generations and show a distinct preference for pop music—to the distress of some of their elders. Western dancing was banned after the end of the Vietnam War until 1986, but both the ballroom and disco versions are now popular again. Karaoke has also penetrated most of the urban centers.

A classical Vietnamese ensemble includes a variety of stringed instruments. Some of them are familiar to Westerners, especially if they have visited China, but others are uniquely local. There are also instruments to provide the rhythm: for classical theater, drums, gongs, and horns are added. In the north, the traditional music tends to be lively, while in the south it is more soulful.

In the traditional Vietnamese theater, everything is kept as simple as possible, somewhat along the lines of Peking Opera. There is no stage scenery, curtain, or special lighting effects. Any furniture will have a symbolic meaning. The roles, the actions of the characters, and even the makeup are all carefully regulated and highly stylized, and are instantly recognizable to the audience no matter what the play. Most of the dramas are legendary and tragic, but the northern part of the country does have some tradition of comedy.

There is also a form of theater that is more down to earth than the classical one, which extols traditional virtues and presents themes familiar to audiences in their daily lives. The musical accompaniment, settings, extravagant costumes, and lighting effects are also more vivid and exciting, so an audience for such a performance is constantly in uproar.

Nha Nhac ("Elegant Music" or "Ceremonial Music")

Nha nhac is the traditional Vietnamese court music that was performed at annual ceremonies and special events, such as coronations, funerals, or official receptions, by large-scale ensembles of highly trained and skilled court musicians. There are also a number of intricate court dances. Both musicians and dancers wear elaborately designed costumes.

Nha nhac became the official court music under the Nguyen emperors and was an esssential part of

the rituals of the royal palace. Influenced first by the Ming Chinese and then the Champa cultures, it is a rich and varied synthesis of genres and repertoires with a high degree of improvisation. Today it is still performed in the old capital of Hue. *Nha nhac* was recognized in 2005 by UNESCO as a Masterpiece of the Oral and Intangible Heritage of Humanity.

Literature

Buddhist *bonzes* (monks) were the first to produce poetry and prose, almost invariably Chinese in form. However, there were Vietnamese forms of literature that were passed down orally from one generation to the next. Gradually, the Chinese influence was broken. In 1527, Portugese missionaries came to Vietnam and began using latin script to transcribe the Vietnamese language. The romanized form of Vietnamese, *Quoc Ngu,* was completed by the French Jesuit missionary Alexandre de Rhodes in the seventeenth century, but the feudal administration prohibited its use until 1930, when it became dominant, replacing the old Vietnamese writing that used Chinese characters. It has been the official script since 1945.

Poetry is particularly prized by the Vietnamese, the poems expressing their innermost feelings, depicting the closeness of Vietnamese life to nature, and vividly describing the history, customs, and culture of the country. Modern poets are carrying on this tradition and exploring new ground.

The most famous poem in Vietnam was written by Nguyen Du in the eighteenth century. In 3,254 verses, it tells the tragic story of a beautiful girl named Thuy Kieu. In order to save her family, she gives up the man she loves to marry a rogue who then leads her into prostitution. Later, she becomes a Buddhist nun and finally a victorious revolutionary's wife; the message being that, through all adversity, one must retain a pure heart. This poem is very popular and has been called the "soul" of the Vietnamese people. Today some people use it for fortune telling by dipping into the text at random and interpreting the verse they've alighted on.

Some of Vietnam's classic literature, both poetry and prose, is becoming increasingly available in foreign translation, and it is well worth picking up a volume or two to help understand the Vietnamese psyche.

Traditional Crafts

The Vietnam War demonstrated the ingenuity of the Vietnamese people in catering to the demands of the

times, symbolized, for example, by the souvenir helicopters made of Coca-Cola cans or the embroidered jackets with crazy English-language slogans on the back that are still available in the street markets of Ho Chi Minh City. But some old traditions have been revived to provide the souvenir hunter with something substantial to take home. Metallurgy has a long history in Vietnam and the Vietnamese are particularly fond of gold, either

in its unworked form or in jewelry, as decoration and long-term investment. Vietnamese have also worked in lacquer for many centuries, and many shops in the major cities display lacquer work of varying quality.

Vietnamese ceramics are also a good buy. During the Vietnam War in particular it seemed that everyone wanted to take home one of the country's specialties: a ceramic elephant. Leather goods and textiles have been produced for a long time and are on display everywhere. Vietnamese craftsmen are also adept at engraving horn, including converting the ordinary turtle's shell into a gleaming work of art.

SHOPPING

In Hanoi, a memorable shopping expedition involves wandering through a labyrinth of narrow streets in the old part of the city, where the traditional trades are still carried on, each in an area still identified in the names of the thoroughfares—Silk Street, Gold Street, and the like.

A typical feature of Vietnamese life is the small shop house, where the family lives at the back and the front is open to the passing trade. Clothing of every description, electrical products, medicines, and traditional handicrafts spill out onto the pavement. The streets are thronged from morning to night by a vast press of pedestrians, making movement by any form of motor vehicle extremely difficult.

Many of the old traditional markets still exist in the big cities and it is great fun to wander through them and engage in haggling with the vendors. But, in the South in particular, as we have seen, mini-marts and large shopping centers are beginning to change the face of shopping.

ESSENTIAL CERTIFICATION

"Antiques" can be found everywhere, but the foreign buyer may run into trouble when seeking to take items out of the country. There are regulations on what constitutes a protected item that cannot be exported, but these are somewhat ambiguous, so careful checking is required before purchase. It might be wise to consult in advance with the local Vietnamese Embassy on the current rules, and possibly see a list of what can or cannot be taken out of the country. The other question is whether the antiques are genuine or not. There is a flourishing industry in producing fakes, as in many other countries, and even a certificate of authentication is no guarantee, as this too can be faked.

Although the fixed price system is beginning to gain ground, there are still many places where bargaining is part of the process and even a pleasurable way of buying something. The Vietnamese, however, are extremely tough bargainers with a vast fund of patience, so it is hard for the foreigner to come anywhere near winning the game. If time is not a problem, it pays to shop around, and the prospective buyer should always be prepared to walk away if the bargaining process is getting nowhere.

Officially, transactions should be carried out in the local currency, the Dong, but many of the informal traders will seek to get paid in foreign currency, especially US dollars. They may also offer to change money, but this can be risky, as the money changer may cheat at the visitor's expense.

PLACES TO VISIT
Decades of war did terrible things to many of Vietnam's old attractions, but there is still a great deal to see and enjoy around the country.

Ho Chi Minh City
The amazing thing about Ho Chi Minh City is that the city center is virtually unchanged from its days as Saigon, the city of tree-lined boulevards and smart shops that earned the title of "Paris of the East." Many of the public buildings in this area were constructed in the years around 1900 and are in the old French style.

A sharp contrast is provided by Cho Lon, meaning "big market." Once a twin city of Saigon,

it is now the "Chinatown" of Ho Chi Minh City. It has long been the home of the Chinese community and is a great place to eat and shop by day or night—but not recommended for those who suffer from claustrophobia!

To escape from the incessant noise and bustle of daily life, city residents head for Vung Tau, near the mouth of the Saigon River 70 miles (112 km) away by road. This is a popular seaside resort, although the beach is not considered as fine as that further north at Nha Trang (where a range of mountains provides a perfect picture frame for the white sands and coral reefs) and the area has been somewhat spoiled by oil drilling in the coastal waters.

Tay Ninh is also worth a visit (see discussion of the Cao Dai on pages 59–60), and war buffs will want to visit Cu Chi, 40 miles (64 km) from the southern metropolis, where a former Viet Cong tunnel complex has been meticulously restored.

Visitors to Cu Chi have the chance to crawl through a labyrinthine, claustrophobic tunnel network to experience the life of Viet Cong guerillas hiding from American attack. A similar network has been opened up in Vinh Moc, Quang Tri Province, near the former demilitarized zone. Even parts of the Ho Chi Minh Trail, the legendary wartime jungle logistics route from north to south along the border with Laos and Cambodia, have become tourist attractions.

Mekong Delta

From Ho Chi Minh City, there are options to tour the Mekong Delta, perhaps by rental car or, for the more adventurous, by a succession of local buses.

The Mekong Delta is the rice bowl of South Vietnam as well as a garden of tropical fruits such as mango, mangosteen, and rambutan. The Delta

is carpeted with rice fields, green gardens, houses, canals, waterways, and floating markets. Visitors can take a cruise from the city of Can Tho along the Mekong River to Siem Riep in northwestern Cambodia to visit Angkor Wat. The Mekong Delta is the background for the famous semi-autobiographical romance *L'Amant* (*The Lover*) by Marguerite Duras, which was turned into a movie with the same name directed by Jean-Jacques Annaud.

Islands

There are two big islands in the south. Phu Quoc in the Gulf of Thailand is as big as Singapore. It is a beautiful island with sandy beaches and a jungle in the center. Phu Quoc is famous for producing fish sauce and black pepper. Visitors here can go fishing, scuba diving among the coral reefs, or relax in a small inhabited islet.

The remote archipelago of Con Dao in the southeast was once a penal colony where first the French and later the Americans incarcerated and tortured political prisoners and Viet Cong fighters in the infamous "tiger cages"—cells that were concrete pits with steel grates at the top. Con Dao today is a tourist destination thanks to the natural beauty of its landscape, deserted sandy beaches, and secluded resorts.

The Central Highlands

In the central highlands, and best reached by air, is Da Lat, 4,920 feet (1,500 m) above sea level, a former summer retreat for emperors and the

country's elite,
whose pine
forests and
cool breezes
are a welcome
change from
the enervating
conditions
on the plains.
Kontum,
Pleiku, and Ban Me Thuot are other places of
interest in the highlands, where there are ethnic
minorities with their own distinct cultures. Elephant
riding is now a popular tourist attraction.

The Central Coast

On the coast, Da Nang, site of one of the biggest
American air bases during the Vietnam War, offers
good beaches and excellent seafood, but is also a
convenient jumping-off point to reach the ruins of
My Son, once the religious and intellectual center
of the Cham kingdom (see page 23) from the fourth
to the thirteenth centuries. The Cham museum
in Da Nang contains
stone statues and
artifacts taken from
archaeological sites.

In central
Vietnam, the city
of Hue boasts the
Imperial City, where
emperors held court
for centuries. Much

of it was destroyed by the fighting that took place during the Tet Offensive in 1968. The former royal citadel, constructed in 1805, took a battering but has been restored.

Hanoi

Built around a series of charming and picturesque lakes, Hanoi sprawls out into the Red River Delta, where a dike protects the city from the former threat of devastating floods. Once outside the old city, concrete tends to rule, for the market economy has transformed the landscape and the government has had trouble regulating the breakneck growth. Hanoi contains some wonderful colonial architectural treasures, however, and great efforts have been made to preserve the exteriors of the old French colonial villas while modernizing the interiors to function as high-quality homes or offices. The central areas with their tree-lined streets and lakes are a delight for the visitor and should be explored on foot.

One might also visit the mausoleum of Ho Chi Minh, a structure built in defiance of the leader who spurned the idea of any grandiose monument, while the Military History Museum enables one to get a view of the conflict from "the other side."

Northern Vietnam

Much has been written about the spectacular Bay of Ha Long ("Dragon's Den"), which has been named a Unesco World Heritage Site. This is an area of sea north of Hanoi that is studded with thousands of islands and islets covering an area of approximately 1,000 square miles (2,590 sq. km), created probably by past volcanic activity. It is said to be named after a huge sea monster of such dimensions that it causes a change of tide when entering or leaving its den. The action of the waves over many centuries has created innumerable fantastical shapes, with crags sticking up like pyramids, towers, pillars, monumental arches, and giant porticoes, all given fanciful names by the local people. Cruises of Ha Long Bay are now available.

culture smart! **vietnam**

Heritage sites:

Ha Long Bay

Phong Nha – Ke Bang National Park

Cultural Heritage:

Complex of Hue Monuments

Hoi An Ancient Town

My Son Sanctuary

Central sector of the Imperial Citadel of Thang Long, Hanoi

Citadel of the Ho Dynasty

Mixed Heritage site:

Trang An landscape complex

Intangible Cultural Heritage forms:

Nha nhac, Vietnamese court music

The space of gong culture in the Central Highlands

Ca tru singing

Quan ho Bac Ninh folk songs

Giong Festival at Phu Dong and Soc temples

Xoan singing in Phu Tho Province

Worship of Hung Kings in Phu Tho Province

Art of Don ca tai tu music and song in south Vietnam

Documentary Heritages:

Buddhist Sutra woodblocks of Truc Lam Zen at Vinh Nghiem Pagoda

Woodblocks of the Nguyen Dynasty

Stone stele records of royal examinations of the Le and Mac dynasties

Imperial Records of the Nguyen Dynasty

Global Geological Park

Dong Van Karst Plateau

The most interesting hotel in the area, the Ha Long Bay Hotel, is an old colonial building overlooking the sea, which achieved fame when the French actress Catherine Deneuve stayed there for weeks while making the film *Indochine*. There is usually a waiting list for rooms, however.

There is an especially picturesque road running from Hanoi through the main tourist centers of the higher regions along the Chinese border. It goes through such mountain towns as Lang Son and Cao Bang. At Sapa, an attractive mountain village near the border, inhabitants still practice centuries-old traditions. Many are members of the Hmong, Dao, and Thai hill tribes. From here you can climb Fanxipang—the "rooftop of Indochina."

chapter seven

TRAVEL, HEALTH, & SAFETY

GETTING AROUND

Traveling around the country is part of the adventure of visiting Vietnam. Great efforts are going into improving the transportation infrastructure, but one stills needs time and some patience to get around the country by land. Many of the main cities are linked by flights operated by the national airline, but if you choose this method od travel you will miss so many of the delights unfolding below.

By Rail

During the war, the old railway line that snaked down the length of the country was heavily damaged by American air raids in the north and the demolition of bridges and track by Viet Cong sapper squads in the south. Happily, the line has now been repaired and it is possible to travel between Hanoi and Ho Chi Minh City, stopping at Hue, Da Nang, and Nha Trang along the way.

However, do not expect a speedy trip. The train meanders along at a steady pace, and it takes between 40 and 52 hours to complete the entire

1,079-mile (1,736-km) journey. For this reason a
sleeping berth is strongly recommended. There
are four options: "soft sleeper" (four berths), with
or without air-conditioning, and "hard sleeper"
(six berths), again with or without air-conditioning.

By Western standards, fares are remarkably
cheap, especially since the higher fare structure
for foreigners was abolished in 2002 so that now
everyone pays the same. Apart from the difference
between "hard" and "soft" in terms of luxury,
the fare structure also includes different rates
according to the position of the bunk (top, bottom,
or middle). There are also non-sleeping carriages
similarly with hard and soft seats. Children ages
five to nine pay half fare on the trains, while those
over ten must pay full fare.

By Road

Long-distance buses still take the intrepid traveler
to most of the places of interest in Vietnam in due

course, but it can be an extremely crowded and not necessarily very pleasant journey. Today air-conditioned coaches ply the same routes. Private rental cars are available, but they can be prohibitively expensive (say, US $40–50 a day) if used for more than the occasional must-see expedition.

BOOK AHEAD

Advance reservations are essential for train travel, and separate tickets and reservations must be obtained if you plan to interrupt your journey at any station en route. Bookings can also be made in advance via the Internet or through some travel companies. The Web site www.seat61.com provides interesting information on train travel.

For really leisurely travelers, it is quite feasible to travel to Vietnam by train from Europe. The first stage is to Moscow, and then on the Trans-Siberian and other trains to Beijing. From there, there are several routes through southern and southwestern China that eventually reach Hanoi. The route through the mountains from Kunming in Yunnan is extremely picturesque—and hair-raising. At the time of writing, construction was also under way of further international railway lines linking Vietnam with Thailand, Malaysia, and ultimately Singapore. Again, such a journey requires extensive forward planning and advance reservation.

WHERE TO STAY

Until the mid-1990s, both Hanoi and Ho Chi
Minh City suffered from a severe shortage of
international-standard hotels, but then the
pendulum swung the other way with a glut of
rooms as a result of new construction and not
enough visitors. The big-name hotels—the
Hilton, Marriott, and Intercontinental—are not
cheap, though they are less expensive than in
Europe. However, many visitors on tight budgets
prefer to look around for one of the many "mini-
hotels" that have sprung up in the more liberal
economic environment.

With land costs high, these hotels tend to be
tall and thin, typically one room wide and two
deep, and often operated by a single family.
Though the number of rooms available may be
limited, they still offer most of the basic comforts,
such as an en suite bathroom, telephone,

television, and even a refrigerator. What may not be on offer is food cooked on the premises; but it is easy to find a decent restaurant down the street, and many of these small hotels often have arrangements with a nearby establishment to have meals, especially breakfast, brought in for guests.

HEALTH
Staying Healthy

Providing they take basic commonsense precautions, few people experience serious health problems in Vietnam. Malaria is now a problem in only a few remote areas, and mass immunization programs have helped to reduce the incidence of infectious diseases drastically. Nevertheless, basic vaccinations are a wise precaution, and the traveler should take along some basic medicines for dealing with upset stomachs and other minor problems; in addition, it would be wise to take from home any prescribed medications rather than rely on their availability at the destination.

It is best to assume that drinking water is risky throughout Vietnam. Bottled water, soft drinks, and beer are freely available and cheap. Vietnamese food is nearly always cooked from fresh ingredients, and an upset stomach is more likely to come from a change of diet than from some bacterial infection.

The proportion of live births and life expectancy are both rising as health care standards improve, but Vietnam still faces many health challenges. In particular, HIV/AIDS is increasing, fueled by growing drug abuse and unsafe sex. However, the country has scored some remarkable successes, notably being the first to eradicate an outbreak of the often fatal respiratory disease SARS in the spring of 2003. This, however, was followed by a serious outbreak of bird flu. This infected large numbers of chickens and made the jump into humans with fatal consequences in a number of cases (admittedly those coming into close contact with live birds); it now seems to have become endemic to the region.

Most of the infrastructure in Vietnam was built during the colonial period, and is now in desperate need of replacement. Some of the rivers and lakes in urban areas are little more than open sewers, and concentrations of heavy metal and other industrial pollutants are well above safe levels in some areas, with obvious consequences for human health.

Public health facilities are good in the big cities, limited in other urban areas, and almost nonexistent elsewhere. Many of Vietnam's hospitals are in antiquated colonial buildings. Equipment is basic, and medical staff often lack necessary skills and experience. Patients have to pay for treatment and medication—poor people are exempted. However, a new employee medical national insurance scheme has been launched and is proving popular. Foreigners are considered to be rich and, therefore, able to pay a level of medical fees far beyond the means of the local population. Any visitor, therefore, would be well advised to take out comprehensive medical insurance to cover all eventualities, including emergency evacuation from the country should an extremely serious illness develop. Having said that, in both Hanoi and Ho Chi Minh City there are private five-star hospitals.

Weather Dangers
The major health dangers really come from the weather. In the south, for instance, a tropical sun can quickly burn the skin even if the sky is overcast, and the high humidity can be extremely enervating (one reason why many people retire for a siesta after lunch). As sunstroke is also a big risk, a wide-brimmed hat that will shade the back of the neck as well as the eyes is recommended.

Heavy sweating caused by the high humidity can quickly lead to dehydration, so visitors need to drink plenty of water each day. In some coastal areas in central Vietnam and in the low-lying valleys in the northwest, the hot and dry weather due to the föhn effect encourages rapid sweat evaporation. The result is that the body may lose water and its mineral balance may become disrupted, leading to exhaustion.

The image of Vietnam as a tropical country, however, may lead one to overlook the fact that, in the north, especially in the mountainous areas, the winter is very cold, possibly encouraging frostbite, pneumonia, bronchitis, and other respiratory diseases. Rapid changes in the weather during the period of seasonal transition can also have an impact on problems associated with advancing age, such as high blood pressure and cardiac arrest.

The Rest Break

One of the biggest worries I had in traveling around Vietnam was the timing of natural "rest breaks." Don't expect to find public toilets scattered around the landscape, whether in the city or in the countryside. And there are no highway service stations, either, where the traveler can gain relief. In the cities, one should have no reservations about popping into a major hotel or office building in search of such facilities, however.

On a long road trip through northern Vietnam a few years ago, I took my lead from my guide, who, having a weak bladder, was always stopping our car to relieve himself at the roadside without any compunction, proudly demonstrating his command of English slang by announcing his intention! One acquaintance of mine always takes medication to reduce urination on journeys, but I prefer to reduce the amount of liquid intake during the day to achieve this end (although this must be balanced by the need to replace fluids lost in the heat). However, if stomach trouble strikes, treat it immediately and reduce traveling as much as possible until it is under control!

Vietnamese Medicine

Recently, much study has gone into developing a unified theory of Vietnamese medicine drawing on three old traditions that coexisted for centuries. *Thuoc Bac*, or "Northern Medicine," was heavily influenced by traditional Chinese medicine (TCM), especially by the belief in Yin–Yang force interactions and the need for balance between the two. The body, it was argued, was intimately linked to external forces, so that good health depended in large part on tuning internal functions to the environment, as well as building defenses against disruptive changes. Disease was defined as impairment of the overall balance between external and internal, physical and moral forces.

As with TCM, *Thuoc Bac* practitioners rely for diagnosis on a mixture of visual inspection, auditory perception, questioning the patient, and taking the various pulses. The main question to be settled by the diagnostician is: does the illness emanate from within the body as a result of poor physical maintenance or emotional strain, or is it the result of external forces, such as seasonal change or inappropriate intake of food or drink, disrupting the system? The next stage is to determine whether the disease is superficial or deep-seated and whether it is of a "hot" or "cold" nature. Drugs would then be prescribed to induce sweating, expectoration, defecation, urination, vomiting, heat reduction, or heat increase depending on the diagnosis.

The second native tradition is *Thuoc Nam*, or "Southern Medicine," which relies heavily on tropical plants and animals native to Vietnam and generally uses ingredients readily available locally and involving a minimum of processing. Knowledge of various peasant remedies is passed on from one generation to the next.

Whereas the first two medical traditions are secular and naturalistic, the third, spiritual healing, contains religious, even magical elements. It involves dealing with harmful spirits, ideally preventing them from entering the body to cause trouble in the first place. Practitioners believe humans have three "souls." To lose one brings mental and physical disorders; unconsciousness comes with the loss of two; and death with the loss of all three.

Many of the old remedies came back into favor, of necessity, during the First (French) and Second (United States) Indochina Wars when the medical services were heavily disrupted, and the government today is working on trying to harmonize all three traditions, drawing on their best features and combining these with some Western medical knowledge to create a system of medical theory suitable for the country's conditions and present state of development.

SAFETY AND SECURITY
Care on the Roads

Vietnam has about 6,250 miles (10,000 km) of roads, most of which suffered from war damage and neglect. A few years ago, some 40 percent were rated as "poor" or "very poor." Many bridges are also somewhat dilapidated. Upgrading and repair have been under way for some time, but it may be a while before a decent road network is in place.

High speeds are impossible on most roads, although that does not stop local drivers from trying. The basic requirements are one foot hard on the accelerator and one hand permanently depressing the horn to clear a path through the hordes of cyclists and motorcyclists, often loaded down with bags

of rice or other produce—not to mention whole families (children in front of dad, mom behind, demurely sitting sidesaddle)—oxcarts, locally made tractors built at low cost for durability not sleek looks, and pedestrians reluctant to surrender the space they have gained.

Do Not Hesitate!

There are no crosswalks in Vietnam. People cross the road wherever they want. A word of advice to foreign pedestrians: stopping in the middle of the road is dangerous. The trick is to look straight ahead and keep going. Do not stop, and the vehicles will avoid you.

On the open highway, usually every few yards, one is confronted by an onrushing truck or passenger bus, in either case invariably heavily overloaded and tilting at an alarming angle. Fine judgment is required to give way at the last possible moment, avoiding collision by inches. Wrecks along the roadside testify that this good judgment is not always present.

Crime and Begging

In recent years there has been an upsurge in crime in both Ho Chi Minh City and Hanoi, much of it petty and opportunistic. Pickpockets on buses are common in Hanoi. Major streets in the center of Ho Chi Minh City, particularly around the big hotels where foreigners congregate, attract pickpockets, thieves, and muggers. A favorite technique is for a motorcycle to swoop down on an unwary pedestrian at the roadside. The biker's passenger snatches the briefcase, handbag, or shoulder bag (it's claimed some can even strip the watch off a wrist in a twinkling) and the bike disappears into the traffic at high speed.

This applies to both day and night. Especially at night, it may also be inadvisable to travel by the ubiquitous *cyclo*, the pedaled or motorized bicycle rickshaw. Some visitors have been harassed, forced to pay well over the agreed upon fare on reaching their destination, or taken on a detour to be mugged while engaged in what they thought was a relaxing way to see city life.

When it comes to witnessing thieves in action, city dwellers tend to turn a blind eye, convinced it is none of their business but something the government should sort out. The police, too, may heave a sigh when the short-term visitor arrives full of complaints—after all, the paperwork will remain to complicate the officer's life long after the tourist has left.

Aggressive begging is common both in the cities and the countryside and it can be very persistent. Gradually, with the passage of time, one will see fewer badly maimed war veterans trawling the streets for handouts. Also extremely persistent is that juvenile pest, the shoeshine boy, and the swarms of street children who hang on to you are not above picking your pocket if they see the chance to do so. Much of this problem is, of course, due to poverty, and both the government and international aid organizations have been working hard in recent years to reduce the levels of poverty, to the extent that it is now down to below 30 percent of the population. One may feel pity for the children, but it is more than likely that they are working for others and that any money you give will not benefit them to a great extent.

The only advice one can offer is that you keep your wits about you at all times when in a public place. It may sound somewhat foolish to say so, but try not to act too much like a tourist, especially a rich one! When one compares the situation with that in many other countries, Vietnam is a comparatively safe place to visit.

BUSINESS BRIEFING

VIETNAM'S NEW-LOOK ECONOMY

In 2015, the Vietnamese celebrated the
fortieth anniversary of the end of the war that
reunified the country. For some, the war has
left a misleading image of Vietnam as a country

peopled by peasant farmers and
utterly destroyed. But Vietnam's
economy is now among the
fastest-growing in the region,
with annual growth of about
7 percent, leading some foreign
businessmen to believe it is
accelerating on the same path as
South Korea and the other East
Asian "tiger economies." While
exports are booming thanks to
a demand for traditional items
like seafood, silk, and timber
products, the country is also
attracting foreign investment
in high-tech areas such as cars
and electronics. Vietnamese companies are
becoming more competitive on the regional stage
and will surely follow their Chinese and Japanese
counterparts onto the world stage in due course.

Reunified Vietnam was a poor, densely populated country that had to recover from the ravages of decades of war, the loss of financial support from the old Soviet bloc, and the rigidities of a centrally planned economy. From 1986 to 1996 substantial progress was achieved from an extremely low starting point: growth averaged around 9 percent annually from 1993 to 1997. The Asian financial crisis caused a temporary setback from which recovery began only in 2000.

Since the Communist Party elected a new leadership in 2001, the government has reaffirmed its commitment to economic liberalization and has moved to implement the structural reforms needed to modernize the economy and to produce more competitive, export-driven industries. The US–Vietnam Bilateral Trade Agreement came into force near the end of 2001, and Vietnam joined the World Trade Organization in January 2007. Membership in ASEAN has also helped to mesh the Vietnamese economy into expanding regional structures.

Doi Moi Promotes Breakthrough

The turning point for Vietnam came in 1986 when a new set of leaders followed China's example and abandoned Marxist economic dogma, embracing instead the free market. The new policy, which was called *doi moi*, meaning "renovation," encourages wealth-creating businesses. Few people have objected to the change because it has been delivering rising living standards that help mute any opposition to the Communist Party.

As in China, one essential element of the new policy has been the privatization of state-run enterprises. This, however, has been marred to some extent by cronyism and large-scale corruption. The ensuing severe warnings from the World Bank led the government to take firm action, arresting or dismissing senior officials in several ministries. There are concerns that abuses of this kind could slow or even derail the liberalization process unless the government acts decisively.

MAKING INVESTMENT EASIER

In an effort to make it easier for foreign investors to set up business in Vietnam, Hanoi (Ministry of Planning and Investment) and Ho Chi Minh City (Department of Planning and Investment) each launched Internet development projects for business service agencies in 2001. The two Web sites are designed to serve as the first point of contact for potential investors, especially foreigners. The sites are interactive with rich content.

In Hanoi, the Ministry of Planning and Investment (MPI) creates commercial laws and regulations, approves investments for projects that meet a certain monetary value threshold, and provides general information on economic and business conditions. The Ho Chi Minh Department of Planning and Investment adheres to investment laws established at the national level and issues investment licenses for projects deemed too small for the MPI to process. Both agencies issue investment licenses and government documents certifying that an investment project is in line with national development goals.

An application for an investment license typically must be accompanied by supporting documentation (for example, feasibility study, corporate background, and other related documents). Companies can proceed with other government formalities (business registration, labor certifications, and municipal-level agency compliance) only after receiving the license. For a long time, one of the biggest problems for investors—and a potential financial disincentive— has been bureaucratic delays in issuing licenses, and the new services are designed to overcome this blockage and to fight corruption.

DOING BUSINESS

Personal contacts and recommendations are very important in Vietnam.

The most important business ritual is the business meeting, and many of these will be required before anything can go forward, since face-to-face discussions, rather than telephone calls or letters, remain the way that most things actually get done. If a deal goes sour, parties are often left with little or no legal recourse. Only the relationship remains. These personal meetings also allow the participants to gauge each other and develop a sense of trust and understanding. In many ways the same applies in other Asian countries such as China and Japan.

FAKERS AND PIRATES

The biggest problem facing foreign businesses investing or trading in Vietnam is brand counterfeiting and copyright piracy. The Vietnam Anti-Counterfeiting and Trademark Protection Association reports that the most commonly mimicked goods are clothing, cosmetics, medicines, home appliances, electronic products (especially cell phones), cement, music and video discs, and motorbikes. In 2004 alone, Ho Chi Minh City investigated at least two hundred cases in which the intellectual property rights of Honda were allegedly violated. The computer industry says Vietnam leads the world in software piracy: Microsoft, for example, believes that an estimated 92 percent of the computer software available in the country involved pirated versions in 2004.

According to Huynh Tan Phong, Director of the Ho Chi Minh City Market Watch Department, existing laws and regulations overlapped or were contradictory or vague, making it difficult for law enforcement officials to fight the flood of fake and imitation goods. The number of officers skilled in handling intellectual property cases was also insufficient. In addition, existing legislation only covered cases where fake goods caused great financial damage or harm to consumers' health and interests, the official pointed out.

> Recognizing the damage counterfeiting could do to the country's ability to attract foreign business investment, the government, in early 2005, authorized the creation of a new association, operating under the control of the Ministry of Planning and Investment, specifically designed to detect counterfeits and protect intellectual property rights on behalf of foreign-invested enterprises.

Vietnamese business meetings, however, tend to be relaxed affairs, with less of the formality that one encounters particularly in Japan and to a lesser extent China. Exchanges of gifts are part of the business culture. After the formal working session, it's very useful to have a more relaxed business evening meal where you can drink, unwind, talk about family, wife, and children, and create a relationship of trust and ease, which will improve the negotiating atmosphere.

SETTING UP THE MEETING

Meeting the right party is essential. Too often, investors or traders team up with the wrong party or the wrong contact person early on and then are frustrated later when things get bogged down. To avoid this problem, it is vital to do some homework, getting information from other businesspeople, reliable consultants, and trusted Vietnamese contacts. Wherever possible, get a trusted intermediary to arrange an appointment, or obtain a letter of introduction from a mutual friend or acquaintance.

Failure to get a proper introduction can result in the other party not taking you seriously or even refusing the appointment. This is true even for representatives of large companies. Information on foreign companies is not always readily available in Vietnam, so the other party may have little means of gauging your company's reputation apart from the recommendation of those who introduced you.

If you are forced to set up an appointment without any introduction, don't just phone and ask for a meeting. The best way is to send a letter requesting an appointment, including some information about your company. This can be followed up after a few days with a phone call. Without a third-party introduction it is likely there will have to be a few extra meetings to establish that essential element of trust, and, even with an introduction, the process of getting acquainted will occupy some time before you can get down to business. The main thing to remember is to be patient while the element of confidence is built up.

In Vietnam it is not common to commit to meetings a long time in advance. Generally, meetings will be confirmed at most one week prior to the appointment. With high-ranking officials, the meeting may be confirmed only one or two days beforehand, or sometimes at even shorter notice. Although this makes it difficult for potential investors planning a trip, it is a reality in Vietnam. Visitors should reconfirm their meetings one or two days ahead, and then call an hour or two before the meeting to ensure that the scheduled time has not been usurped by another party.

Businesspeople with plenty of experience on the ground warn that meetings tend to take a lot longer than one might anticipate, so it is not advisable to fill the day with too many appointments and tight deadlines. Generally speaking, in the North people are more cautious and circumspect in their replies. In the South businessmen are more decisive and direct (which may explain why business activity in the South is more dynamic).

Generally, it is best to schedule meetings in the morning, Monday through Friday. Afternoons are sometimes reserved for more administrative work, whereas Saturdays are considered holidays in most administrative agencies. Many government offices and companies have weekly meetings either on Monday or on Friday afternoon, making it difficult to schedule an appointment at that time as well.

Business Dress
In business first impressions are important. Today, businesspeople in both North and South are very style conscious and will evaluate you on your appearance. Brand labels and smart accessories will make a good impression.

AT THE MEETING
At the beginning of a meeting, business cards should be exchanged with everyone in the room before any discussions have taken place. Unlike

the Japanese custom, it is not necessary to be terribly formal (that is, handing over the card with two hands and a deep bow), but politeness suggests it is better not to sit down until the opposite principal has done so. Note that while it is very easy to obtain impressive business cards in Vietnam, this does not guarantee that the company is legitimate or that the person is credible. If you have a business card that is in English and Vietnamese, it is good etiquette to present it with the Vietnamese side facing up.

Tea drinking is an essential part of the ritual (although some hosts may offer you a choice such as water or a soft drink), and, again, one should wait for the senior member on the other side to begin drinking before following suit. A few sips for politeness' sake will be quite sufficient; if you empty the cup, it will automatically be refilled.

It is very important not to rush to a discussion of the issues you came to speak about. It is polite to wait for the Vietnamese party to raise the matter for which the meeting was called. In the meantime, talk about other matters such as the economy, your enjoyment of your trip to Vietnam, mentioning how pleased you are to meet them, and so forth. This time can also be well spent by introducing yourself and your firm. This introduction is important to the Vietnamese, who are often reluctant to commit themselves to anything until they know a little about you.

Those intending a long-term commitment to Vietnam should try to learn the language, although more and more of the younger generation in government and business tend to speak at least some English. If you are forced to use an interpreter, in conversation always face the person you are addressing and try not to talk directly to the interpreter.

It is considered a good idea to let your Vietnamese counterpart speak uninterruptedly for a fairly long stretch. The advice is not to question him or her immediately on the points you think ought to be dealt with there and then. It is far more polite and effective to make notes, bringing up queries when it is your turn to speak.

You can be direct without being *too* firm, even though the other side may not be doing so. There can be many reasons other than deviousness in negotiation why the Vietnamese counterpart cannot give a straight answer—including the need to check with his or her political masters for approval first.

As a good host, the Vietnamese party will rarely initiate the closure of the meeting. Instead, it is expected that the guest will respect the time limit for the appointment, especially with a busy government official, so it's best to confirm this, say with a secretary, in advance.

THE DECISION-MAKING PROCESS

The decision-making process really depends on whom you are dealing with. In one sense, it is easy to deal with a private businessman or woman who is operating close to the "front line" and can make quick decisions and implement them. One has a clear idea of whom one is dealing with and there is little need to understand any labyrinthine office politics. At the same time, however, private companies don't always have much influence on the network of contacts within government, both central and local, that can open doors and smooth over difficulties. Dealing with a company in the state or semipublic sector may well be time-consuming to begin with, but it can often help cut down on red tape. Companies in the public sector are always more closely attuned to the nuances of policy change and often know about them in advance of those in the private sector.

The further one goes down the chain of command in government structures, the greater the chance of being slowed down by the complicating factor of corruption. The central government may issue relatively clear guidelines, but they get muddied in implementation. This inevitably complicates the decision-making process. A Vietnamese business executive who seems to be stalling and unwilling to make a decision may, in fact, just be wearily accepting that the process is far more complex than the foreign visitor might realize.

The Australian government's briefing for businesspeople heading for Vietnam suggests that, when a problem arises, it is best to go to the relevant party—an official, a joint venture partner, or whomever—and point out the problem together with a number of potential solutions, with tact and respect. If one points out only the problem but offers no solution it may take a long time to resolve the problem, since the other party is obliged to create a solution. So, providing a number of realistic and equitable options allows the official or partner to merely review them for fairness and not to lose face.

BEING CALM AND NONCONFRONTATIONAL

When a Vietnamese person does not understand something that is said, it is very common for them to smile. They will rarely tell you they do not understand. If it is clear they do not understand, do not confront the issue directly as this may cause them to lose face. Instead, apologize for being unclear and try to explain it a different way. With officials or businesspeople, you have to do this indirectly.

Always remember that, no matter how great the provocation, your stature will be diminished if you show any sign of irritation or anger. Raising one's voice or becoming angry is considered a sign that the individual lacks self-discipline, creating a highly embarrassing situation for the person being shouted at. The Vietnamese, like other peoples in Asia, set great store by "saving face." They are very skilled in detecting the real attitudes of others through tone of voice and body language and react accordingly.

CONTRACTS AND FULFILLMENT

Early investors in postwar Vietnam—
companies who entered in the 1990s—faced
many heartaches, none more galling than the
discovery that the contract they had signed
provided them with very little legal protection
against anything that might go wrong. To put
it as kindly as possible, some of this stemmed
from the relative business inexperience of the
Vietnamese. A repeated problem, for example,
was that rules would be changed after a contract
had been signed and, when applied retroactively
to cover that particular agreement, would make
it unworkable. There were also cases where a
foreign investor thought they had a contract
guaranteeing exclusivity in a particular area,
only to discover the Vietnamese partner trading
with someone else in the same commodity.

The situation has improved more recently,
but it remains true that, the further one moves
away from the major urban conglomerations in
South and North, the greater the potential for
contractual problems. This is why, as already
mentioned, it is so important to establish a close
personal relationship with one's Vietnamese
partner(s) and to proceed very cautiously to
"dot the Is and cross the Ts" as much as possible.
Fulfillment can also depend on one's keeping a
watchful eye on things, so it is no use signing a
contract and going home expecting everything
to run smoothly thereafter. "Out of sight, out of
mind" is a good motto to remember as a warning
in this regard!

TRADE UNIONS

The trade union movement is essentially an arm of the government, but that has not prevented it from showing a degree of independence, particularly when it comes to foreign investors. Ever since the mid-1990s, they have been facing a strong union drive for more legal protection, higher wages, and better working conditions. What has mitigated the impact of this is the fact that every potential complainant in the workforce knows that there are probably many people waiting outside the factory gate or office door eager to take his or her place.

A labor code came into force on January 1, 1995, giving workers the right to form trade unions and to strike for the first time. It also provided for the formation of labor courts and a mechanism for arbitration involving business, union, and government. The operation of the code has been patchy, especially in the private sector, however. One problem is that the government is trying to balance the need to pacify workers with the need to encourage investment.

The Vietnamese have a strong work ethic and are good employees if treated well. But they are not entirely passive. Strikes and work-related disputes have been reported on a regular basis, but most of these seem to come down to perceived ill-treatment of the workforce by management: low wages, long hours without overtime pay, refusal to grant medical and other social benefits as stipulated by law, and even physical abuse by employers.

chapter nine

COMMUNICATING

LANGUAGE

Scholars fail to agree completely as to the origins of the Vietnamese language. Some have placed it in the Thai or Mon-Khmer group, while others have plumped for the Indo-Malay group or the Australo-Asiatic family of languages. Nguyen Dinh Hoa, an influential figure at one time in the Saigon Faculty of Letters, believed the Vietnamese lexicon had many nouns in common with the Cambodian or Khmer language. This is especially true of nouns dealing with parts of the body, members of the kinship system, farming tools, species of flora and fauna, and some other categories. He also argued that Vietnamese used many of the same final consonants as Thai and, like Thai, used various levels of pitch and tone.

New words were added to the language when Vietnamese territory was dominated by the Chinese, while more recent influences, including that of the French, have also contributed words that have then been "Vietnamized" and given local pronunciations.

Although Vietnamese in one form or another might have been spoken in the past, no one has been able to determine with any certainty what

sort of written form it might have taken until it adopted Chinese characters, or *Chu Nho* (scholars' script), in the ninth century. Chinese characters came into use in all official transactions, correspondence, and literature. This written language, however, was different from the spoken language, and, as still happens today, people across East Asia (for example, the Chinese and the Japanese) could write to each other and be understood but couldn't communicate verbally with the same facility.

Vietnamese scholars and writers, however, began to seek a means of communicating in a uniquely Vietnamese way. Gradually some of the native speech began to be represented in phonetic form (something the Japanese also did with their *hiragana* and *katakana* scripts to

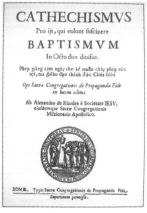

supplement the Chinese characters or *kanji*), but only in literary works. During the seventeenth century, however, Catholic missionaries began arriving from various parts of Europe, and they looked for some linguistic tool to convey their ideas to potential converts. Led by the French Jesuit scholar-missionary Father Alexandre de Rhodes, a system of romanized writing, known as *Quoc Ngu* (national language), was developed after twelve years of study. In 1649, de Rhodes completed a Vietnamese–Portuguese–Latin dictionary. *Quoc Ngu* was finally recognized as the official language in 1920 and began to be used in all primary schools in the country in 1945.

Speaking Vietnamese
Like Chinese, Vietnamese is a heavily tonal language, creating all sorts of possibilities for the hapless foreign beginner to mispronounce a word and thus completely change the meaning, to the delight of the Vietnamese (although they try to hide their mirth out of politeness).

There are six tones in the north and five in the south, and a simple word like *ma* can, for example, mean "horse," "mother," "ghost," "rice seedling," or "tomb," depending upon the way it is said. It is interesting that exactly the same word also means "horse" and numerous other things in Chinese, depending upon the inflection.

Mind Your Language
Mispronunciation can be a minefield. "Cho Lon," we have seen, means "big market." If "Lon" is mispronounced as "Lọn" it means "pig," or can even be misconstrued as the feminine organ.

There are twelve vowels and twenty-seven consonants in Vietnamese. The language is noted for its lack of inflectional endings or the changing of the form of a word to indicate number, gender, and so on. Translated into English, a Vietnamese sentence might read, "Today Ben give I six pencil." Modifiers always follow the noun, adjective, verb, or adverb that they modify, for example, Continent Asian, village small, expensive most. As Ann Caddell Crawford observed in her Vietnam War-era classic *Customs and Culture of Vietnam*: "Many words are left out. One might compare a Vietnamese sentence with a thrifty telegram; all words that can be left out are omitted. It may have an understood subject or no subject at all."

Previous generations of (North) Vietnamese students studied Russian in keeping with the country's ideological allegiances, although many older people could speak French. Now, English is the language of choice in university studies.

Minority Languages
Vietnam's ethnic minorities, especially the mountain people in both north and south, have

an entirely different linguistic tradition, which they have managed to preserve through all attempts to absorb them into the mainstream culture. Each tribe, in fact, may speak a different language, so that sign language has to be used when members of different tribes encounter each other.

There are two main groups: Mon-Khmer and Malayo-Polynesian. The Mon-Khmer languages are used by many small ethnic minority groups living in different parts of Southeast Asia. The Malayo-Polynesian languages, as the name might suggest, are used in some parts of Indonesia and different islands in the Pacific. The tribes using the former include the Hmong and the Montagnard peoples, while those using the latter include the Jarai, Hroi, Raday, and Cham. However, there are also small tribes living in the remote mountain regions of northern Vietnam close to the Chinese border who also use dialects obviously of Tibeto-Chinese origin.

FACE-TO-FACE COMMUNICATION
The Naming System
What to call Vietnamese people is a potential trap for the unwary. Vietnamese names consist of a family name, a middle name, and a personal or given name, in that order. An example is the name Nguyen Van Hung. As explained below, the middle name indicates a male, while the given name in this case means "courage." Thus,

this is a man of the Nguyen family line whose family at his birth wished to see him to grow up to become a person of great courage. He should be addressed as Mr. Hung and not Mr. Nguyen.

As this example shows, one addresses another person using the given name, not the family name. There are a few exceptions to this general practice. For political reasons, to express their elevated their status, Ho Chi Minh was known as President Ho (or Uncle Ho) and the first South Vietnamese president Ngo Dinh Diem was called President Ngo. In the old days, only the king was referred to by his dynastic name. Referring to a king by his given name was punishable by imprisonment or even death.

There are about one hundred family names for the whole population, but only a few are frequently used, such as Nguyen, Le, Tran, Pham, Phan, and Truong. This is another good reason why Vietnamese are not called by their family names, because it would simply be too confusing. A Vietnamese woman retains her own family name after marriage.

Parents often choose given names for their children that reflect their aspirations and ideals. Almost any word in the Vietnamese language can be used as a given name. Some of the common names are words denoting qualities and virtues (Trung—fidelity, Hung—courage, Liem—integrity); the seasons (Xuan—spring, Thu—fall); flowers (Hong—rose, Lan—orchid); fruits (Nho—grape, Le—pear), or natural phenomena and celestial bodies (Tuyet—snow, Van—cloud,

Nguyet—moon). Girls' names are frequently chosen from words denoting virtues or things that are beautiful, sweet, fragrant, or melodious.

Vietnamese middle names are used for various purposes. They are used to differentiate a man's name from a woman's name, since practically no Vietnamese names are exclusively masculine or feminine. Common middle names for women are Thi and, less often, Nu. So, Nguyen Van Hai is a man and Nguyen Thi Hai is a woman. These days, however, young people tend to drop the gender indicator. Middle names can also serve to differentiate one branch of a family from another. In this case, the same middle name is shared by all those members who share a common ancestor. In other cases, the middle name indicates the generation level; all those of the same generation have the same middle name.

Meeting and Greeting

Social custom dictates the use of different words when greeting someone depending on their age, sex, and status, although the stumbling foreigner will almost certainly be forgiven any linguistic transgressions. The various greetings are:

chao ong to an older or important man, such as a grandfather

chao anh to a younger man, say, a brother

chao chu to a man younger than your father but older than you, such as an uncle

chao ba to an older or important woman. such as a grandmother

chao chi to an older woman

chao co to a younger woman
chao em to a child, male or female; someone
subordinate to you, or someone close, such
as a husband
chao ban to a friend of your own age

One should call Vietnamese people "Mr.,"
"Mrs.," or "Miss" (or by their professional title if
they have one) until invited to address them on a
first-name basis. Unless the person concerned has
become totally Westernized, this is likely to take
some time.

Direct Questions, Straight Answers

Although Vietnamese people often avoid giving a
straight answer, this does not stop them from asking
foreigners very direct questions about their age,
marital status, family background, and even the cost
of the clothes they are wearing. This stems from a
natural curiosity about life outside their country
and things that few Vietnamese have yet had a
chance to see (although this is fading in the major
cities, where foreigners are now a common sight,
and so is television). One can choose to answer
such questions frankly or simply turn the
questions aside in a gentle, joking manner.

Vietnamese seldom use a direct approach in
their dealings, since this would indicate a lack of
tact or delicacy. Especially frustrating for visitors
can be the tendency to avoid saying "no" even
when a negative answer would seem appropriate
in Western eyes. One should therefore particularly
avoid asking negative questions.

BODY LANGUANGE

The custom of handshaking, formerly considered barbaric by the Vietnamese, is now widespread through Western influence. Urban men will generally shake hands and offer a conventional greeting. Women, especially in the countryside, still shy away from shaking hands, so it is best not to offer to shake hands with a woman unless she offers her hand first.

It is rare now to see Vietnamese in urban areas bow when they meet each other, unless they are of the older generation. In formal gatherings,

NONVERBAL COMMUNICATION

Nonverbal communication plays a far more important role in Vietnamese than in Western society.

- You will quickly discover that a smile or silence invariably replaces "thank you" and is not a sign that one has said or done something wrong. For example, if one offers someone a compliment, a verbal expression of thanks would suggest a lack of modesty by the recipient (unless it is to vehemently deny the truth of the compliment); a smile or a blush is a normal response.

- Winking in any circumstances is indecent; pouting is considered dismissive, and an expression of disdain.

- What one does with the hands is also crucial. Placing them in the pockets or on the hips at religious places, and sometimes in the country areas, one may see the people clasp their hands together in a prayerlike gesture and bow slightly, however.

Don't Touch

Many Westerners are tactile by nature, but this can get you into trouble in a relatively conservative society like Vietnam. It is considered highly impolite to touch anyone of the opposite sex, no matter how innocent the motive, even to giving a little pat of encouragement. Certainly, touching

suggests arrogance or lack of respect. Folding one's arms is respectful, however. A pat on the back is disrespectful, especially to anyone older or senior in status; pointing at a person during a conversation is also considered rude.

- Holding hands is acceptable with someone of the same sex, but should be avoided in public with the opposite sex.
- Beckoning should be avoided because in some circumstances it can be rude or even threatening. In particular, when calling to someone, never beckon with an upturned finger: this is considered very impolite and to make such a gesture would indicate an air of authority or superiority over the person being summoned. If you must silently signal for someone to come toward you, do so by using the whole hand with the palm turned down.

anyone on the head would be considered a personal insult to the individual and perhaps even their ancestors, for the traditional Vietnamese belief was that this was where the spirit resided.

Another old belief now fading into history was that a genie resided on the shoulder and it was undesirable to disturb it by touching. Should one accidentally touch a person's shoulder, the antidote was immediately to touch the other one to offset any possible bad luck.

Eye Contact

In traditional Vietnamese culture, looking into somebody's eyes, especially when the person is of a higher status (in age or in social or family hierarchy) or of a different sex, usually expresses a challenge, or deep passion. Therefore, if a Vietnamese appears to be avoiding direct eye contact it is an indication not of shiftiness or deviousness but of personal modesty and respect for the other person.

THE MEDIA

Domestic newspapers and television and radio stations remain under strict government control. Although journalists are occasionally able to report on corruption by government officials, direct criticism of the Party is forbidden. Foreign media representatives are required to obtain authorization from the Foreign Ministry for all travel outside Hanoi.

Printed Media

The main Vietnamese-language newspapers are the *Nhan Dan* and the army newspaper *Quan Doi Nhan Dan* in Hanoi, and *Giai Phong* in Ho Chi Minh City. In English, Hanoi has the *Vietnam News*, while Ho Chi Minh City has the *Saigon Times Daily*. The main English-language magazines are *Vietnam Investment Review* and the *Vietnam Economic Review*, both obviously business-related. Most Vietnamese newspapers have an English online version.

From women's magazines analyzing beauty and home decoration to tabloid newspaper exposés of gangsterism and government corruption, the media are beginning to flourish as never before; but taboo topics remain. Writers and editors who call for political pluralism or criticize government policy take huge risks. But, while the media certainly exercises some form of self-censorship, it does seek to discuss serious issues and present all sides of the argument. Various government departments often use the media to argue their own point of view and there have been cases of policies and legislation being amended or withdrawn after vigorous media debate. Certainly the younger generation, with access to the Internet and foreign broadcasts, expects more from the domestic press, and this will almost inevitably help to expand the boundaries in the years ahead.

Television and Radio

Today there are 786 media agencies owning 1,016 publications, including newspapers and magazines, both printed and online. There are 67 broadcasters, including Vietnam National Television (VTV), and 75 international channels are available on cable TV.

Vietnam has also lauched two communication satellites.

The Internet

The government maintains strict control over access to the Internet. It blocks Web sites considered objectionable or politically sensitive and strictly bans the use of the Internet to oppose the government, "disturb" national security and social order, or offend the "traditional national way of life." In August 2004 the Ministry of Public Security created a new office to monitor the Internet for "criminal" content.

Despite these controls, the social media have becone very popular in Vietnam and people use Facebook and blogs both to share ideas and to facilitate business.

MAIL AND TELECOMMUNICATIONS

Vietnam has put considerable effort into modernizing and expanding its telecommunication system, but its performance continues to lag behind that of its more modern neighbors. All provincial exchanges are digitalized and connected to Hanoi, Da Nang, and Ho Chi Minh City by fiber-optic cable or microwave radio relay networks; main lines have been substantially increased, and the use of cell phones has grown rapidly.

Two Russian satellites over the Indian Ocean provide Vietnam with good international telephone links.

Postal services are fairly reliable in the main cities, although delivery may be rather slow by Western standards. Mail sent out of the country via post offices poses little problems, but the visitor might not want to place too much reliance on efficient delivery of incoming mail. Mail addressed to the major hotels is considered the most reliable.

CONCLUSION

For a long time in the mid to late twentieth century "Vietnam" was a word with negative connotations, indicative of much that was wrong with the world. It meant Cold War, Big Power confrontation, the threat of global Communist domination, political and military brinksmanship, the destruction of millions of lives, the end of the beautiful dream of President Lyndon Johnson's "Great Society"—the list is endless. Today, as this book has sought to demonstrate, it conjures up a land full of hope, with areas of great natural beauty, a hardworking people determined to build an advanced country equal to any on earth, and an ancient culture carefully preserved and kept vividly alive.

Although there may still be imperfections, especially as regards a modern infrastructure—providing all the creature comforts a pampered international traveler expects—once the main cities have been left behind this, too, can have its charms. The visitor prepared to take the rough with the smooth should have little difficulty in adapting to conditions at large. With understanding and a fair bit of patience, most people should find a visit to Vietnam a delightful, memorable experience that will expunge all the grim images of the past and leave behind a pleasant taste and a desire for more.

In Vietnam, you will find a people full of contrasts, as you might expect from a country going through a period of rapid and far-reaching change. In the cities, everyone seems to be in a frenetic hurry to get where they are going, both physically and philosophically; in many parts of the countryside, on the other hand, the pace of life and the traditional attitudes reflect an earlier era where patience and stoicism were the abiding virtues. Together, these qualities create a delightful kaleidoscope of cultural difference that will reward the thoughtful and inquiring visitor.

Further Reading

Business
Binh Tran-Nam et al. (eds). *The Vietnamese Economy: Awakening the Dormant Dragon*. London: RoutledgeCurzon, 2002.
Murray, G. *Vietnam: Dawn of a New Market*. London/New York: China Library and St. Martin's Press, 1997.

Guides
Curry, J., et al. *Passport Vietnam* (Passport to the World Series). Novato, California: World Trade Press, 1997.
Jealous, V., and F. Mason. *Lonely Planet: Vietnam*. Melbourne/Oakland/London/Paris: Lonely Planet Publications, 2003.
Kalman, B. *Vietnam Culture* (Lands, Peoples and Cultures Series). New York: Crabtree Publishing Co., 1996.
Rough Guide to Vietnam 4. London, New York: Rough Guides, 2003.

History
Taylor, K. *The Birth of Vietnam*. Berkeley, California: University of California Press, 1983.

Language
In-Flight Vietnamese. New York: Living Language, 2006.

Literature
Denenberg, B. *Voices from Vietnam*. New York: Scholastic, 1997.
Thich Nhat Hanh. *Call Me by My True Names*. Berkeley, California: Parallax Press, 1999.

Vietnam Today
Ashwill, M., with Thai Ngoc Diep. *Vietnam Today: A Guide to a Nation at a Crossroads*. Yarmouth, Maine: Intercultural Press, 2005.
Lamb, D. *Vietnam Now: A Reporter Returns*. Cambridge, Massachusetts: Public Affairs, 2002.
Templar, R. *Shadows and Wind: A View of Modern Vietnam*. London: Penguin, 1998.

Vietnam War
Baker, M. (ed). *Nam: Vietnam War in the Words of the Men and Women Who Fought There*. London: Abacus, 1992.
Del Vecchio, J. *The Thirteenth Valley*. New York: St. Martin's Press, 1999.
Herr, M. *Dispatches*. London: Picador, 2002.
Kaputo, P. *Rumors of War*. New York: Henry Holt, 1977, 1996.
Karnow, S. *Vietnam: A History*. Harmondsworth: Penguin, 1984.
Maclear, M. *Vietnam: The Ten Thousand Day War*. London: Thames Methuen, 1981.
Mason, R. *Chickenhawk*. London: Corgi Adult, 1984.
Windrow, M. *The Last Valley: Dien Bien Phu and the French Defeat in Vietnam*. London: Weidenfeld & Nicholson (hardback), 2004/Cassell Military (paperback), 2005.

Index

Acknowledgments

I would like to dedicate this book to all veterans of the Vietnam War—on both sides.